Content Area Literacy Strategies That Work

Content area teachers are now being tasked with incorporating reading and writing instruction, but what works? In this essential book from Routledge and AMLE, author Lori G. Wilfong describes ten best practices for content area literacy and how to implement them in the middle-level classroom. She also points out practices that should be avoided, helping you figure out which ideas to ditch and which to embrace.

Topics covered include . . .

♦ Building background knowledge quickly
♦ Using specific strategies to scaffold focus while reading
♦ Using small group reading strategies to bring personal response and accountability to the content
♦ Understanding items that make reading in different disciplines unique
♦ Teaching content area vocabulary in meaningful ways
♦ Making writing an authentic process through daily and weekly assignments
♦ Planning and teaching effective informational and argumentative pieces

Each chapter includes Common Core connections and practical templates and tools. The templates are available as free eResources so you can easily print them for classroom use.

Lori G. Wilfong is a former middle school language arts teacher, current Associate Professor in Middle Childhood Education at Kent State University, frequent conference presenter, and forever supporter of teachers working to weave literacy into their classrooms.

Content Area Literacy Strategies That Work

Do This, Not That!

Lori G. Wilfong

Routledge
Taylor & Francis Group
AMLE
NEW YORK AND LONDON

First published 2019
by Routledge
52 Vanderbilt Avenue, New York, NY 10017

and by Routledge
2 Park Square, Milton Park, Abingdon, Oxon, OX14 4RN

Routledge is an imprint of the Taylor & Francis Group, an informa business

Library of Congress Cataloging-in-Publication Data
Names: Wilfong, Lori G., author.
Title: Content-area literacy strategies that work : do this, not that /
    Lori G. Wilfong.
Description: New York : Routledge, 2019. | Includes bibliographical
    references.
Identifiers: LCCN 2018048165 (print) | LCCN 2018061551 (ebook) |
    ISBN 9781351240895 (ebook) | ISBN 9780815375036 (hbk) | ISBN
    9780815375043 (pbk) | ISBN 9781351240895 (ebk)
Subjects: LCSH: Content area reading—Study and teaching (Middle
    school) | Language arts—Correlation with content subjects. |
    Reading comprehension—Study and teaching (Middle school) |
    Common Core State Standards (Education)
Classification: LCC LB1050.455 (ebook) | LCC LB1050.455 .W545
    2019 (print) | DDC 372.47/6—dc23
LC record available at https://lccn.loc.gov/2018048165

ISBN: 978-0-8153-7503-6 (hbk)
ISBN: 978-0-8153-7504-3 (pbk)
ISBN: 978-1-351-24089-5 (ebk)

Typeset in Palatino
by Apex CoVantage, LLC

Visit the eResources: www.routledge.com/9780815375043

To the teachers of Maple Heights City Schools . . . your dedication, willingness to try new strategies, and ability to see what kids are capable of inspires me every day.

Contents

Setup of This Book

To describe each item on the **Do This, Not That** list, this text has been set up with a specific structure:

♦ A description of the research behind each "Do This" item

♦ Strategies that update traditional instructional practice for each item on the list

♦ Common Core State Standards that correlate with each strategy

♦ Action steps and reflection items for each item to help spur your instructional change!

eResources

The templates and handouts in this book are also available as free downloads on our website, so you can easily print and distribute them to your students. To access them, visit our website at www.routledge.com/9780815375043 and click on the eResources tab.

Meet the Author

Lori G. Wilfong, PhD, began her career as a naïve (and yet know-it-all) teacher at a middle school in East Los Angeles. Two days into her job teaching English to sixth-, seventh-, and eighth-grade English Language Learners, she realized how much she didn't know about teaching. This set the course for the rest of her career: To learn as much as she could about motivating adolescent readers, reading in the content areas, young adult literature, and differentiated instruction. A frenzy of advanced degree getting followed, including a master's in Reading Specialization and a doctorate in Curriculum & Instruction, both from Kent State University. She worked as a literacy coach and a literacy specialist in rural and urban districts in Northeast Ohio before landing in the department of Teaching, Learning, and Curriculum Studies at Kent State University at Stark, Ohio, where she currently is an Associate Professor, teaching courses in literacy to both preservice and practicing teachers.

Lori continues to hone her skills in school districts, working with teachers with one goal always in mind: to make all students love reading. She previously authored *Vocabulary Strategies That Work: Do This—Not That!*, published in late 2012, *Nonfiction Strategies That Work: Do This—Not That!*, published in spring 2014, and *Writing Strategies That Work: Do This—Not That!*, published in spring 2015. She lives in Munroe Falls, Ohio, with her husband, Bob.

DO THIS	NOT THAT . . .
Build background information quickly	Spend so much time building background information that students have no reason to read the actual text
Help scaffold focus while reading with specific strategies	Hand out a reading without assisting students to focus on important concepts
Use small group reading and learning strategies to bring personal response and accountability to the content	Make all reading and learning opportunities whole class
Address discipline-specific content reading strategies	Ignore the items that make reading in different disciplines unique
Use content area vocabulary in meaningful ways	Assign vocabulary to study without attending to why and how words are selected and practiced
Make writing an authentic process in every classroom	Force writing in your classroom
Promote daily writing strategies to strengthen thinking in the discipline	Write only "big" writing assignments once or twice a semester
Implement slightly larger weekly writing strategies to encourage comprehension and synthesis in the discipline	Write only "big" writing assignments once or twice a semester
Plan and teach one "big" informational piece per semester	Assign a vague informational research report
Plan and teach one "big" argumentative piece per semester	Assign a vague argumentative paper

Chapter 1

Build Background Information Quickly

As a fourth-grade teacher to a majority of English Language Learners, my colleague Stephanie worked extra hard to teach both content and context to her students. Social Studies was proving especially difficult: "We focus on Ohio history which is engaging but my students have such little knowledge about the United States, let alone the state we reside in!" She looked dolefully at the textbook that she usually uses to tackle the topic. "I can't just announce that we are going to start reading. I have to bring them up to speed on state, national, and world contexts so it makes sense." She sighed and thumped the textbook onto a back table. "Any ideas on how to do that and teach my standards in 47 minutes?"

Why Is This Item on the List So Important?

Stephanie is describing a scenario that all teachers face: To help a student comprehend a text or topic, we must build background knowledge. But in order to build background knowledge, we must use precious class minutes to activate what students already know so that they are ready to learn more. And in some cases, like Stephanie's, students are blank slates; for many (often complicated) reasons, our students have little or no knowledge to build on.

Diving into a topic does a disservice to our students and our content. These authors stated it well: "Put simply, the more you know about a topic, the easier it is to read a text, understand it, and retain the information" (Neuman, Kaefer, & Pinkham, 2014, p. 145).

Nonfiction text, the genre that most content area teachers use in their classrooms, requires background knowledge built around vocabulary (addressed in Chapter 5) and concepts (Price, Bradley, & Smith, 2012). As students progress in their learning, each standard is predicated upon learning in previous grade levels. Take Stephanie's example from the anecdote at the beginning of this chapter: If a student has been in Ohio for their schooling, in third grade they will learn about community laws and how they fit into the vision of the state. If students are new to the state, or country for that matter, she needs to think about all the information they might need in order to access the current grade level's standards.

One of the most difficult aspects of background building is the time it takes to do it well. Teachers walk a precarious line here—if I give too much background to my students, they have no interest in reading or learning about the topic. And if I spend too little time, I risk moving on with instruction that my students are not ready for.

> *"Do this, not that" principle #1: DO Build background information quickly. DON'T spend so much time building background information that students have no reason to read the actual text.*

To Get Started

Awakening comprehension. Building background knowledge lays the foundation for eventual comprehension of a text or topic. This was once explained to me by someone who specializes in brain-based research by giving the analogy of a computer hard drive: When you write a new document on your computer and go to save it, you have to decide how you are going to organize this file on your computer. Which folder should it go in? You eventually tuck it away into a folder that makes sense to you. And yet, if you were to go through the files on my computer and make sense of my organization, it might not make sense. Our brains work in a similar way. When we learn something new, our brains are rifling through the "folders" on our "hard drive," trying to find a connection for this new information to something we already know. Once it finds this connection, a synapse is literally formed—your brain is growing! But if you don't have a piece of knowledge in your brain for this new information to latch onto, the new information can be lost. By building background knowledge with our students, we are building and accessing their brain "folders" to help them retain new information.

I can show this through a sentence:

The note was sour because the seam split.

Just by forcing you to read this sentence, I have activated the folders in your brain. You are rifling through your own knowledge, trying to make sense of what seems to be a wacky sentence. When I show this to learners, I get the following responses to the question, "What can this sentence possibly mean?"

♦ "I think of milk because of the word 'sour.'"

Milk is a popular answer because sour milk is something most of us have experienced at some point.

♦ "Wine comes to my mind, like if one of the "notes" of the wine went bad."

My wine drinkers often respond with this (sometimes embarrassed that they thought of wine!).

♦ "Maybe someone was singing and their pants split!"

These are my choir people.

Generally, with each response, I can tell what kind of background knowledge each group has and how they used it to make sense of the sentence. So, when I show the sentence again, I add in a key word:

The *bagpipe* note was sour because the seam split.

Right then, your brain just said aha! It rifled through your folders and brought up a visual of a bagpipe player walking in a parade. You possibly heard in your mind the playing of that bagpipe. And then you were able to imagine what that bagpipe might sound like if the seam split. Sour, indeed!

Direct and indirect experiences. Robert Marzano (2004) states there are two ways to build background knowledge with students: direct and indirect experiences. Direct experiences like museum visits, travel, previous work in laboratory settings, and field trips offer powerful venues for students to build background knowledge (feel free to include that sentence the next time you have write a proposal for a field trip for your classroom). Our students' direct experiences vary widely; we have students who travel and participate in cultural events while other students' lives are narrowed to the walls of where they live and go to school. These individual experiences influence how students are able to process and extract information from a text (Kintsch, 1988).

A teacher recently shared an example of this from his high school social studies classroom:

> We were discussing Hitler marching his troops down the Champs de Elysee and through the Arc de Triomphe in Paris and one of my students jumped out of her seat as if her pants were on fire! "I've been there," she screamed, digging in her backpack to get her phone out. She scrolled through her photos and ran up to the front of the room to show me a selfie of her in front of the Arc. This student, who had been pretty uninterested before, was all of sudden the center of attention and *paying* attention because of that connection.

When I asked the teacher if many of his students traveled like that, he shrugged his shoulders: "Sadly, no. And some of the other kids were pretty jealous that she had been there."

It is through indirect experiences that we can give other students access to content and build background knowledge. While it may not seem as powerful as a selfie under the Arc de Triomphe, indirect experience is how most of us build our background knowledge. Pictures, videos, skimming, social media, and discussion are all authentic ways that scientists and historians learn about a topic before diving into a dense text.

The tried and the true. There are some basic ways to build background information that we have all used before, including videos, webquests, and the good ol' KWL. There is nothing wrong with these strategies and if you are already using them with success, continue! I have also written about a few pre-reading strategies in a previous book, *Nonfiction Strategies That Work* (Wilfong, 2014) that accomplish the same background building goal: Tea Party and Book Box.

Instructional Practices to Update

Updated Strategy #1: Carousel Walk (Lent, 2012)

One of the best places to access background knowledge is your students, themselves. As illustrated in the anecdote above about the selfie, when our students make personal connections or share their experiences with others, we are building background knowledge in an enjoyable, motivating way. But because we can't wait for random acts of connection, we sometimes have to create these opportunities, ourselves.

A carousel walk (Lent, 2012) allows student to do two things they love most, group work and graffiti. This strategy allows students to preview content in a motivating manner while building background knowledge through the collective understanding of their classmates. Here's how to do it:

1. Prior to the teaching of a unit or topic, identify five or six main concepts or terms that students will encounter. For example, for an eighth-grade science unit on energy, a teacher identified these six concepts: energy, mass, magnetic field, positive charge, and negative charge.

2. Decide if you want to simply display these words or if you want to find images to show the word, or a combination of both. Depending on your learners, I find images a great way to spark a larger variety of conversations about the topic.

3. Display your words or images on larger pieces of butcher paper. Be sure to leave a large border around the word or image to allow student written response.

4. Hang the butcher paper pieces around the room, allowing space (if possible in a cramped classroom!) between them.

5. Decision time!

   a. Can your students work in groups? Handle multiple voices talking at once? Then place your students in six groups and nominate one person per group to be the leader by handing them a marker. Give each group a different colored marker. Assign each group to a picture or word. Set a timer for three minutes. The group leader writes down anything a group member says about the word or picture (unless it is silly or illogical). When the timer goes off, the groups rotate to the next picture and start the process again, but this time have the previous group's work to use as a starting point. I do find that the number of minutes needed at each picture dwindles as the rotations continue—at some point, there are just not that many words one can write about a picture, word, or quote.

b. Does your class function better as a unit? Then you take the marker and move your way around the classroom while your students stay seated. Write down your students' suggestions for each topic.

6. At the end of the exercise, you have accomplished two things:

a. You have built a shared vocabulary around this topic.

b. You have built background knowledge on this topic.

Figure 1.1 shows an example of a carousel walk from a science classroom.

Updated Strategy #2: Wide Reading (Fisher, Ross, & Grant, 2010)

Wide reading is exactly what it sounds like—allowing a student to explore a topic through multiple texts (Fisher, Frey, & Hattie, 2016; Fisher, Ross, & Grant, 2010). To test a theory that wide reading could be applied to content area classrooms, researchers Fisher et al. asked students to peruse a set of materials in a high school physics class. Class then proceeded as usual—textbook reading,

Figure 1.1 Student Responses During a Carousel Walk

experiments, lecture, etc. Through just 10–12 minutes a day of reading, student knowledge of classroom learning, as measured on a textbook-created assessment, revealed statistically significant improvements (Fisher et al., 2010).

Accomplishing wide reading is gained by curating a set of materials that students can access during class time. This is not the time for complex text; this is the time to bring in picture books, simple articles, and more that students can easily read in a short amount of time. One of the reasons students balk at textbook reading is the dry, dull tone often found in content area textbooks. But set a picture book on a content area topic in front of a student, and the mood instantly lifts.

Before you scoff at the idea of bringing picture books into your middle school or high school content area classroom, stop! When is the last time you really went to see the breadth and depth of picture books, both fiction and nonfiction, that are out there? Many of these books, especially those on science and social studies topics, are full of great facts *and* the engaging pictures that make reading them not a chore (Bintz, 2014).

The hardest part about wide reading is creating the text set. While you don't necessarily have to have an item for each student in your classroom (i.e. 30 students = 30 different items), you do want enough copies of items so that every student is engaged. In fact, I personally found having maybe ten different items with enough copies for every student to have something to read created a bit of mystique when some students picked one item but *really* wanted another (picture books were *way* more popular than the articles—even the articles in full color with pictures!). Your media specialist or local librarian are great places to start: tell them your topic and see what they can find. I also combed through *National Geographic for Kids*, *Time for Kids*, *Ranger Rick*, and accessed Newsela and Tween Tribune (websites that present current events for students at a variety of levels) for engaging articles on the topic of study. Figure 1.2 is a sample text set I created for an eighth-grade social studies teacher about to embark on a unit studying the American Revolution. While

Figure 1.2 American Revolution Wide Reading Text Set

When Washington Crossed the Delware by Lynne Cheney
The Declaration of Independence from A to Z by Catherine Osnorio
Let it Begin Here: Lexington & Concord by Dennis Brindle Fraden
Boston Tea Party by Pamela Duncan Edwards
Ben Franklin's Almanac by Candace Fleming
Katie's Trunk by Ann Turner
George vs. George by Rosalyn Schanzer

I only list picture books here, I find that articles and websites can accomplish the same goal, if you are so inclined!

I know, squeezing that 10–12 minutes of reading beyond your normal classroom activities is hard. But engaging with motivating texts like those mentioned above can make your other classroom instruction easier because of the background information built in your students.

Updated Strategy #3: Using Technology to Reach and Teach the World

When I was a new teacher, I read a book with my students entitled *Summer on Wheels* by Gary Paulsen. This book was about two boys who embarked on a bike ride from East Los Angeles, where I taught, to Santa Monica, where I lived. At the end of the book, the two boys enjoy a day at the beach. When we finished reading, one of the students told me that he wished he could see the ocean. I polled the class and was astonished to discover that only a few of my students had seen the Pacific Ocean, only 16 or so miles away. We spent a class period looking at pictures online (it was the early 2000s; the internet was catching up) and I found that my students were mesmerized looking at these pictures, which in turn sparked their interest in reading about those same places.

While nothing can replace an actual field trip (oh, how I wished I had the funds to take my students to step foot in the ocean!), our virtual field trip, through pictures on the internet, to the Pacific Ocean helped my students to better understand the book we were reading. Today, we have so many resources at our fingertips to help our students explore the world, building background knowledge to tackle the topics in our classrooms. Spending a day on these "trips" is a worthwhile way to support student learning before beginning a unit. Here are a few of my favorites:

1. *Virtual museum visits.* While it may not be possible to fly your students to France, you can virtually visit the hallways of the Louvre to look at ancient Egyptian artifacts before studying Egypt. Or studying dinosaurs? The American Museum of Natural History in New York City has virtual tours of all of its permanent exhibits and even archives past exhibitions. Explore as a class or allow students to "visit" and then share what they learned.

2. *GoogleLitTrips.* Reading a famous piece of literature? This great site has links to books appropriate for several different ages. The files are downloadable and take students on journeys to see where characters or historical figures have been. *The Diary of Anne Frank* (the Holocaust), *The Watsons Go to Birmingham* (American Civil Rights), *The Grapes of Wrath* (the Dust Bowl), and more are all set for you to

take your students to get a geographical context of historical events and ideas mentioned in a variety of books without leaving your classroom.

3. *The Discovery Channel.* Under the name "Discovery Education," virtual field trips on a myriad of topics are available for use in the science and math classroom. I actually bookmark this site because periodically they host "live" field trips where you can stream in to watch something unfold before your eyes. But if you miss it, it will be archived for use at your leisure. Topics include wind farms, Mars, and aerospace facility tours.

Common Core Connection

The strategies discussed in this chapter lay the foundation to meet several of the standards listed in the Common Core Standards for Literacy in History/ Social Studies, Science, & Technical Subjects; however, background building strategies are not meant to be assessed. In all chapters that follow this one, the chapter will end with a list of standards met by the strategies discussed. This chapter purposely leaves them out so that you can focus on stair-stepping your students to the standards, not assessing them.

Action Steps

Building background information can be a great way to engage your students in the study of a topic! It is time to take some action . . .

1. Select a topic for a Carousel Walk: _____
   a. Brainstorm five to six ideas that fit into that topic.

   i. _____

   ii. _____

   iii. _____

   iv. _____

   v. _____

   vi. _____

b. Make a decision—will you provide your students with images, quotes, words, phrases, or all of the above? _____
_____

c. Instructional decision—will you place your students in groups or lead the activity, yourself? _____

2. Select a topic for a Wide Reading text set: _____
_____

   a. Research a list of titles to use to support that topic:

     i. _____

     ii. _____

     iii. _____

     iv. _____

     v. _____

     vi. _____

3. Do any of the technology resources fit with your content area? Are there any other similar resources out there to support building background knowledge with your students in your content area?

_____

_____

_____

_____

_____

_____

_____

Works Cited

Bintz, W. (2014). *Using paired texts to meet the Common Core: Effective teaching across the K-8 curriculum*. New York, NY: Guilford.

Fisher, D., Frey, N., & Hattie, J. (2016). *Visible learning for literacy: Implementing the practices that work best to accelerate student learning*. Thousand Oaks, CA: Corwin.

Fisher, D., Ross, D., & Grant, M. (2010). Building background knowledge: Improving student achievement through wide reading. *The Science Teacher, 77*, 23–26.

Kintsch, W. (1988). The role of knowledge in discourse comprehension: A construction-integration model. *Psychological Review, 95*(2), 163–182.

Lent, R. C. (2012). *Overcoming textbook fatigue: 21st century tools to revitalize teaching and learning*. Alexandria, VA: ACSD.

Marzano, R. J. (2004). *Building background knowledge for academic achievement: Research on what works in schools*. Alexandria, VA: ACSD.

Neuman, S., Kaefer, T., & Pinkham, A. (2014). Building background knowledge. *The Reading Teacher, 68*, 145–148.

Price, L., Bradley, B., & Smith, M. (2012). A comparison of preschool teachers' talk during storybook and information book read-alouds. *Early Childhood Research Quarterly, 27*(3), 426–440.

Wilfong, L. G. (2014). *Nonfiction strategies that work: Do this—not that!* New York, NY: Routledge.

Chapter 2

Help Scaffold Focus While Reading with Specific Strategies

I scanned the seated juniors in front of me. Headphones in ears, hands propping up heads, article in front of them. The teacher at the front of the room called out, "You have ten minutes left; make sure you answer the questions at the end of the article." Every student stopped whatever they were doing, flipped to the end of the article and began working on the questions. The teacher walked back to where I was sitting. "I think the questions just became more important than the actual reading," he said, shrugging his shoulders. "How can I get them to really dig into the text?"

Why Is This Item on the List So Important?

Show of hands here: How many of us commiserate with the students in the scenario above? You were assigned something to read, you weren't really into it, and you used the questions at the end of the chapter or article to help you focus on what you assumed the teacher must think is important. I am going to guess that many of us used this technique as a way to fake our way through an assignment. The problem with this technique is that once we get to college or in a job, there are no questions at the end of the text; we have to read for the sake of mastering the material and must use our own judgement about what we think is important or irrelevant.

In Chapter 1, we honed in on building background knowledge for reading content area texts. In this chapter, we will focus on ways to help students dig into a text.

> *"Do this, not that" principle #2: DO help scaffold focus while reading with specific strategies. DON'T hand out a reading without assisting students to focus on important concepts.*

To Get Started

It was a widely accepted truth in the literacy world that elementary reading focused on learning to read and intermediate reading and beyond that focused on reading to learn (Chall, Jacobs, & Baldwin, 1990). Recently, scholars began challenging that notion, stating that literacy past fourth grade needs to delve into even more complex reading strategies to allow students to effectively tackle the dense texts that are used in content areas (Fang & Schleppegrell, 2016; Houck & Ross, 2012).

Many K-12 literacy programs focus on the cognitive strategies of reading—visualizing, predicting, inferring, etc. (Moje & Speyer, 2008). While these are still good strategies, they are not always enough to help a student access the technical language, structures, and discourse that true content area texts contain (Moje, 2008).

To illustrate this, Table 2.1 shows side-by-side excerpts of a fiction text widely used in elementary basal readers (left) and a section of a high school biology textbook (right).

Seeing these two texts side-by-side really drives home the need to teach content area text differently (Fang & Schleppegrell, 2016). Asking a student to visualize and predict what is happening with the fiction excerpt makes sense! Asking a student to visualize and infer using the ninth-grade biology textbook is incredibly frustrating. Updating our instructional practices to truly match the text we are teaching will help our students grasp the content being taught.

The ultimate goal, of course, is independence. After working with students to integrate these reading strategies into their repertoires, we must then allow students to select and use the strategy that works best for them—just like they will need to do in real life!

Table 2.1 Side-by-Side Comparison of Elementary versus High School Text

The Last Cover by Paul Annixter	McDougal Littell, *9th Grade Biology*, Chapter 4
I'm not sure I can tell you what you want to know about my brother; but everything about the pet fox is important, so I'll tell all that from the beginning. It goes back to a winter afternoon after I'd hunted the woods all day for a sign of our lost pet. I remember the way my mother looked up as I came into the kitchen. Without my speaking, she knew what had happened. For six hours I had walked, reading signs, looking for a delicate print in the damp soil or even a hair that might have told of a red fox passing that way—but I had found nothing. "Did you go up in the foothills?" Mom asked. I nodded. My face was stiff from held-back tears. My brother, Colin, who was going on twelve, got it all from one look at me and went into a heartbroken, almost silent, crying.	Weather and Climate *What is climate?* Weather and climate both involve variations in temperature, precipitation, and other environmental factors. **Weather** is the day-to-day condition of Earth's atmosphere. Weather where you live may be clear and sunny one day but rainy and cold the next. **Climate**, on the other hand, refers to average conditions over long periods. **A region's climate is defined by year-after-year patterns of temperature and precipitation.** It is important to note that climate is rarely uniform even within a region. Environmental conditions can vary over small distances, creating **microclimates**. For example, in the Northern Hemisphere, south-facing sides of trees and buildings receive more sunlight, and are often warmer and drier, than north-facing sides. We may not notice these differences, but they can be very important to many organisms

Instructional Practices to Update

Updated Strategy #1: Using Text Structure to Analyze and Organize Content

I am the first person to go on a diatribe about the overuse of graphic organizers (in fact, I go on one of these rambles for you in Chapter 6). However, as students are reading, it can be helpful to use a graphic organizer to break down content into meaningful chunks.

Text structure analysis appears in the Common Core Standards as early as third grade. This standard is in the category of Author's Craft, asking the student to think about *why* the author set up the article or chapter using this text structure (Table 2.2 presents these five structures). As teachers of older students, we need to build upon this learning.

I wrote about a similar strategy in *Nonfiction Strategies That Work*, the Text Structure Thinkmat. When I first conceived of the strategy, I was thinking about its use in a language arts class, where a great deal of the nonfiction read is composed of a single text structure. It wasn't until I showed the strategy to a group of social studies and science teachers that they pointed out their materials changed text structure from paragraph to paragraph. The textbook excerpt from Table 2.1 illustrates this perfectly: the first paragraph is a compare-and-contrast text structure while the second paragraph is descriptive. To ask students to select and apply one text structure to an entire chapter or article is not only impossible—it is unfair!

Here are the steps for introducing and implementing text structure analysis to your students:

1. Pre-assess student knowledge of text structure. I find so many teachers want to spend weeks re-teaching the text structures but remember, most students have been studying and applying these since at least third grade! A pre-assessment will give you an idea of how in depth your review needs to be. A sample pre-assessment is presented in Figure 2.1.

Figure 2.1   Sample Pre-Assessment of Text Structure Knowledge

Direction: read each passage and identify how the information is being organized.

1. Ice cream is a delicious frozen treat that comes in many different colors and flavors. Two of my favorite flavors are strawberry and chocolate. Though both of these flavors are delicious, strawberry may contain pieces of fruit while chocolate usually will not. Even though more chocolate ice cream is sold across the country annually than strawberry, each flavor tastes great inside of a milk shake.

   a. cause and effect   b. compare and contrast
   c. chronological/sequence/process   d. spatial/descriptive
   e. sequence/process

Figure 2.1   (Continued)

2. The ice-cream shop around the corner from my house has the best ice cream in the city. When you first walk inside, there is a long chrome counter with matching stools extending to alongside the far wall. Right where the counter stops, the booth seating begins. There are lots of old-timey knickknacks on the walls and chrome napkin holders on all the tables. My favorite part of the shop is behind the counter glass, where they keep all of the ice-cream flavors. A rainbow of delicious sugary flavors is kept cool and delicious behind the counter glass.

   a. problem and solution   b. compare and contrast
   c. chronological/sequence/process   d. spatial/descriptive
   e. sequence/process

3. Freezer burn may have wasted more ice cream than sidewalks. If you don't know, freezer burn is when ice crystals form on the surface of ice cream. These ice crystals can ruin the texture and flavor of the ice cream. But you can prevent freezer burn. Since freezer burn is caused when melted ice cream is refrozen, rather than eating your ice cream from the container as it melts, scoop your ice cream into a bowl and put the container back in the fridge immediately. Doing this ought to help you solve your issues with freezer burn.

   a. problem and solution   b. compare and contrast
   c. chronological/sequence/process   d. spatial/descriptive
   e. sequence/process

4. No one knows the true origin of ice cream, but the first published ice-cream recipe appears in *Mrs. Mary Eales's Receipts,* a cook book that was printed in London in 1718. Sometime around 1832, an African American confectioner named Augustus Jackson created multiple ice-cream recipes and invented a superior technique to manufacture ice cream. Ice-cream soda was invented around 1874, but the real breakthrough may have been at the 1904 World's Fair in St. Louis, Missouri, when the American ice-cream cone was unveiled!

   a. problem and solution   b. cause and effect
   c. chronological/sequence/process   d. spatial/descriptive
   e. sequence/process

5. Making ice cream is not easy. Cream and sugar have to first be mixed in a frozen container. Ingredients may be added at this point, if desired. The mixture must be stirred and whipped until the cream and sugar mixture is frozen. Depending on the equipment, this may take as long as an hour. After the ice cream is prepared, it must be kept frozen until it is ready to be enjoyed. Making ice cream is difficult, but most people would agree that it is worth the trouble.

   a. problem and solution   b. compare and contrast
   c. chronological/sequence/process   d. cause and effect
   e. sequence/process

Figure 2.1 (Continued)

6. Have you ever had an ice-cream headache? That's when a painful sensation resonates in your head after eating something cold (usually ice cream) on a hot day. This pain is produced by the dilation of a nerve center in the roof of your mouth. The nerve center is overreacting to the cold by trying to heat your brain. Ice-cream headaches have turned many smiles to frowns.

    a. problem and solution   b. compare and contrast
    c. chronological/sequence/process   d. spatial/descriptive
    e. cause and effect

7. One time my mom and I made ice cream. We added sugar and cream into a big glass bowl. We kept it frozen in the middle of a bigger glass bowl. While it froze, I stirred the mixture with a hand mixer. It was the first time that had I used one and it splattered ice-cream mixture all over the kitchen. The rest of the mixture finally froze, so we ate some ice cream, and then put the remaining portions in the freezer so that it wouldn't get freezer burned. That was a good day.

    a. problem and solution   b. compare and contrast
    c. chronological/sequence/process   d. spatial/descriptive
    e. cause and effect

8. It was the most beautiful banana split that I had ever seen. In the middle of the bowl, there were three scoops of ice cream: chocolate, strawberry, and vanilla. On top of the ice cream were a banana and a thick web of chocolate and caramel sauces. A huge puff of whipped cream covered the sauces and a handful of crushed nuts dappled the whipped cream. On top of it all was a cherry, but I've never liked the soggy squish of cherries.

    a. problem and solution   b. compare and contrast
    c. chronological/sequence/process   d. spatial/descriptive
    e. cause and effect

9. When it comes to making ice cream, you can do it the traditional way, by stirring it in a frozen container, or you can use liquid nitrogen to freeze your mixture. There are some advantages to using liquid nitrogen. Since liquid nitrogen freezes the mixture faster, the crystal grains are smaller, giving the ice cream a creamier texture. The downside is that ice crystals grow faster in ice cream prepared using liquid nitrogen, so it must be stored at much colder temperatures. Both methods produce a distinct texture, and both are delicious.

    a. problem and solution   b. compare and contrast
    c. chronological/sequence/process   d. spatial/descriptive
    e. cause and effect

Adapted from ereadingworksheets.com (2018)

2. Review the five text structures with students, as needed. I find that nonfiction children's books are a great place for review because most of them follow a single text structure and can still be about subject matter, making it easy for students to identify the text structure being used (and for the teacher to stay on the curriculum path they need to be on!). Table 2.2 presents the five nonfiction text structures, along with a graphic organizer students can use to organize the content.

Table 2.2 The Five Nonfiction Text Structures Plus Graphic Organizers

Compare and Contrast	
Cause and Effect	
Spatial/Descriptive	
Chronological/Sequence/Process	
Problem and Solution	

Compare and Contrast:

	Name 1	Name 2
Attribute 1		
Attribute 2		
Attribute 3		

Cause and Effect:
Cause → Effect, Effect, Effect

Spatial/Descriptive:
Central Idea with Fact, Fact, Fact, Fact

Chronological/Sequence/Process:
First → Second → Third [Text]

Problem and Solution:

Problem	Attempted Solutions
Who What When Where Why	1. 2.
Results	

3. The strategy is now ready to be scaffolded onto grade-level text. On a projector, display an excerpt from an article or textbook. Model reading the passage aloud once. Then, show how different sections and paragraphs can be labeled with their text structure. Finally, model applying the correlated graphic organizer with the passage off to the side of the paragraph or section. Modeling these strategies for your students is imperative; it is truly how we invite students into the reading of the complex texts that they encounter in the content areas (Fisher & Frey, 2015).

4. Have students work in groups to break down another section of the text in a similar manner.

5. Have sticky notes available for students to apply the strategy as they wish!

A few notes about this strategy:

♦ This is a way of doing close reading without waving your arms and shouting at your students "We're doing close reading!" Through the multiple readings of the text to apply the strategy, students can't help but read closely.

♦ A graphic organizer is NOT expected for every paragraph or section. As students get more adept at the strategy, they begin to selectively choose which paragraphs and sections to break down using the text structure.

Updated Strategy #2: Demonstrate How Annotation Works with Content Area Texts

Annotating is a common strategy used by English teachers to help students really engage with a text. It accomplishes two things:

1. It helps make the internal conversation that readers have with a text external. Proficient readers automatically have a conversation with a text, punctuated with phrases like "I agree . . ." "Hmmm, I wonder if . . ." "I bet this is going to happen . . ." But instead of just keeping that conversation internal, the reader marks these thoughts on the page, either with a set of symbols (e.g. ! for new idea or * this is important) or with marginalia (Wilfong, 2014).

2. Annotating helps students slow down and pay attention to text. In today's digital age, it is so easy for the mind to wander. Being forced to annotate helps the brain really think about the reading.

Just like with text structure analysis, I taught annotation with a series of symbols that helps facilitate connections between the reader and the text. And, yet again, when I introduced my version of annotating to a group of content area teachers, they reported back that it did not help their students really learn or understand the content they had hoped they would glean from the reading. It turns out that these teachers were absolutely right! The kind of annotating I was teaching was better for fiction texts and the kind of narrative nonfiction that I would use as an English teacher. To really help teach annotation that works in a content area text, a new set of cues is needed.

Zwica and Gomez (2008) updated annotation to work with content area texts using a different series of marks that were more appropriate to the kind of learning they needed their students to do in their classrooms. Different ideas in the text and how the reader reacts to them are each given their own action. Their original work contained 12 actions to be taken by the reader. A group of science teachers I worked with simplified this down to eight to make it more manageable for their students. Table 2.3 presents these annotations (and could be a handout to give to students as they work to master the strategy).

Table 2.3 Content Area Annotations

Text	Action Taken By Reader	Symbol
Headings and Subheadings	Circle	●
Key Content Vocabulary	Box	▬
Other Difficult Words	Triangle	▲
Important Facts or Main Ideas	Double Underline	═══
Supporting Evidence for Facts or Main Ideas	Single Underline	───
Procedural Words	Arrow	➡
Confusing Information	Question Mark	?
Major Conclusion Drawn	Star	★

Just like with the text structure strategy, modeling is key to annotation. Showing and thinking aloud your process as you annotate a piece of text helps students to see how the method works. After students apply the strategy on a text, themselves, discussion can revolve around their annotations:

♦ What key content area vocabulary did you find in the text?

♦ What were some of the important facts you found? What evidence supports them?

♦ Discuss the procedural words with a partner.

♦ What is the major conclusion the author presents?

Updated Strategy #3: Explicitly Teaching How to Find and Generate Main Idea Statements Using a Main Idea Log

Teaching the main idea is MAJOR—if a student is able to identify what a text is mostly about, and then is able to deliver the main idea in a neat package, they have literally won the comprehension battle. I have talked to so many teachers who have complained about the lack of students with adequate summary skills. Beyond the classroom, this soft skill becomes a trait that employers look for and cite as lacking in high school and college graduates (Alexander & Hirsch, 2012).

Summary writing involves four complex processes:

♦ Finding the main idea.

♦ Eliminating the irrelevant information.

♦ Finding sufficient supporting evidence to back the main idea.

♦ Writing up the main idea in a few brief but illustrative sentences.

(Wilfong, 2015)

Main idea and summary appear in the Common Core State Standards as early as first grade, so it is common for teachers to assume that students already have mastered these skills by the time they get to middle school and beyond. But approaching the complex texts of subject areas already saps the brain power of readers; having to apply the complex processes described in summary writing, above, to these difficult texts is like summarizing in a whole new language! This is why re-teaching new and different main idea and summary techniques throughout middle school and high school is important; we are giving students' brains the chance to apply these skills to the language of the discipline they are studying.

There are two main idea/summary strategies that I have written about previously that I have tested across the disciplines with success: SWBST (Somebody/Something, Wanted, But, So, Then) and The Most Important Thing About (Wilfong, 2014).

SWBST is useful when working with a text that has a problem and solution. Students figure who or what the main figure or topic of the text is (Somebody/Something), what the problem is (Wanted), what stands in the way of solving the problem (But), what steps are taken to solve the problem (So), and how the problem is resolved (Then). Table 2.4 presents a template for this strategy (a blank template for the strategy is included at the end of the chapter).

Once students have completed the graphic organizer after reading, they can use it to write a simple, four-sentence summary:

1. Somebody/Something Wanted

2. But

3. So

4. Then

The Most Important Thing About is based on *The Important Book* by Margaret Wise Brown (1949). This simple children's book provides a simple template for summary writing:

The most important thing about _____ is _____.

Supporting Detail #1

Supporting Detail #2

Supporting Detail #3

But, the important thing about _____ is _____.

Is it sophisticated summary writing? No. Does it help students hone in on the main idea and supporting details necessary to support a text? Yes!

Table 2.4 Template for SWBST

Somebody/ Something	Wanted	But	So	Then

Figure 2.2 Main Idea Log in Action

Title of Text:		
"Who" or "What" is this text about?	What is the most important information about the "who" or "what"?	Use the information in columns 1 and 2 to write a main idea statement of ten words or less.
Summary (choose 2–4 main idea statements):		

The final main idea/summary strategy to model and try with students is a Main Idea Log (Wexler, Reed, Mitchell, Doyle, & Clancy, 2015). First developed to help struggling readers, this simple think sheet allows students to read for the who/what of a passage, decide the most important information about that who or what, and then join those two pieces of information to write main idea statements. Similar to both of the two strategies presented above, this strategy allows students to record several different main topics and supporting information by deciding on a final main idea/summary statement after reading. Figure 2.2 presents the template for this strategy (a blank template for the strategy is included at the end of the chapter).

Common Core Connection

The strategies in this chapter support several of the Common Core State Standards for Literacy in History/Social Studies, Science, & Technical Subjects:

Reading Standards (History/Social Studies)

6–8	9–10	11–12
6–8.1 Cite specific textual evidence to support analysis of primary and secondary sources.	9–10.1 Cite specific textual evidence to support analysis of primary and secondary sources, attending to	11–12.1 Cite specific textual evidence to support analysis of primary and secondary sources, connecting

6–8	9–10	11–12
6–8.2 Determine the central ideas or information of a primary or secondary source; provide an accurate summary of the source distinct from prior knowledge or opinions. 6–8.3 Identify key steps in a text's description of a process related to history/social studies (e.g., how a bill becomes law, how interest rates are raised or lowered). 6–8.5 Describe how a text presents information (e.g., sequentially, comparatively, causally).	such features as the date and origin of the information. 9–10.2 Determine the central ideas or information of a primary or secondary source; provide an accurate summary of how key events or ideas develop over the course of the text. 9–10.3 Analyze in detail a series of events described in a text; determine whether earlier events caused later ones or simply preceded them. 9–10.5 Analyze how a text uses structure to emphasize key points or advance an explanation or analysis.	insights gained from specific details to an understanding of the text as a whole. 11–12.2 Determine the central ideas or information of a primary or secondary source; provide an accurate summary that makes clear the relationships among the key details and ideas. 11–12.5 Analyze in detail how a complex primary source is structured, including how key sentences, paragraphs, and larger portions of the text contribute to the whole.

Reading Standards (Science & Technical Subjects)

6–8	9–10	11–12
6–8.1 Cite specific textual evidence to support analysis of science and technical texts. 6–8.2 Determine the central ideas or conclusions of a text; provide an accurate summary of the text distinct from prior knowledge or opinions.	9–10.1 Cite specific textual evidence to support analysis of science and technical texts, attending to the precise details of explanations or descriptions. 9–10.2 Determine the central ideas or conclusions of a text; trace the text's	11–12.1 Cite specific textual evidence to support analysis of science and technical texts, attending to important distinctions the author makes and to any gaps or inconsistencies in the account. 11–12.2 Determine the central ideas or

(Continued)

(Continued)

6–8	9–10	11–12
6–8.3 Follow precisely a multistep procedure when carrying out experiments, taking measurements, or performing technical tasks. 6–8.5 Analyze the structure an author uses to organize a text, including how the major sections contribute to the whole and to an understanding of the topic.	explanation or depiction of a complex process, phenomenon, or concept; provide an accurate summary of the text. 9–10.3 Follow precisely a complex multistep procedure when carrying out experiments, taking measurements, or performing technical tasks, attending to special cases or exceptions defined in the text.	conclusions of a text; summarize complex concepts, processes, or information presented in a text by paraphrasing them in simpler but still accurate terms. 11–12.5 Analyze how the text structures information or ideas into categories or hierarchies, demonstrating understanding of the information or ideas.

Action Steps

Helping students stay focused and understand the big ideas of a text is important! It is time to take some action . . .

1) The five strategies presented in this chapter are all very different. What sequence of instruction do you think will be most beneficial to your students?

   a.

   b.

   c.

   d.

   e.

2) The strategies presented discuss the use of paper texts that students can mark up or the use of sticky notes (in the case of textbooks). If the majority of your texts read are electronic, how could you adapt these strategies for use with those types of texts?

   _____

   _____

   _____

   _____

3) Which of these strategies would support *you* most as a reader? Why?

_____

_____

_____

_____

Works Cited

Alexander, K., & Hirsch, B. (2012). Marketable job skills for high school students: What we learned from an evaluation of After School Matters. *New Directions for Youth Development*, *134*, 55–63.

Brown, M. W. (1949). *The important book*. New York, NY: Harper & Row.

Chall, J., Jacobs, V., & Baldwin, L. (1990). *The reading crisis: Why poor children fall behind*. Cambridge, MA: Harvard University Press.

Fang, Z., & Schleppegrell, M. J. (2016). Disciplinary literacies across content areas: Supporting secondary reading through functional language analysis. *Journal of Adolescent and Adult Literacy*, *53*, 587–597.

Fisher, D., & Frey, N. (2015). Teacher modeling using complex informational text. *Reading Teacher*, *69*, 63–69.

Houck, B. D., & Ross, K. (2012). Dismantling the myth of learning to read and reading to learn. *ASCD Express*, *7*. Retrieved from www.ascd.org/ascd-express/vol7/711-houck.aspx

Moje, E. B. (2008). Foregrounding the disciplines in secondary literacy teaching and learning: A call for change. *Journal of Adolescent & Adult Literacy*, *52*, 96–107.

Moje, E. B., & Speyer, J. (2008). The reality of challenging texts in high school science and social studies: How teachers can mediate comprehension. In K. A. Hinchman & H. K. Sheridan-Thomas (Eds.), *Best practices in adolescent literacy instruction* (pp. 185–211). New York, NY: Guilford.

Wexler, J., Reed, D., Mitchell, M., Doyle, B., & Clancy, E. (2015). Implementing an evidence-based instructional routine to enhance comprehension of expository text. *Intervention in School and Clinic*, *50*, 142–149.

Wilfong, L. G. (2014). *Nonfiction strategies that work: Do this—not that!* New York, NY: Routledge.

Wilfong, L. G. (2015). *Writing strategies that work: Do this—not that!* New York, NY: Routledge.

Zwica, J., & Gomez, K. (2008). Annotating to support learning in the content areas: Teaching and learning science. *Journal of Adolescent and Adult Literacy*, *52*, 155–164.

SWBST

Somebody/ Something	Wanted	But	So	Then

The Most Important Thing About

The most important thing about _____ is _____

_____ .

Detail #1:

_____

_____

_____

Detail #2:

_____

_____

_____

Detail #3:

_____

_____

_____

But, the important thing about _____ is _____

_____ .

 Main Idea Log

Title of text:		
"Who" or "What" is this text about?	What is the most important information about the "who" or "what"?	Use the information in columns 1 and 2 to write a main idea statement of ten words or less.
Summary (choose 2–4 main idea statements):		

Chapter 3

Use Small Group Reading and Learning Strategies to Bring Personal Response and Accountability to the Content

I tapped the arm of the student sitting next to me: "Is there a routine for learning in this room?" The student smirked back. "I guess you can call it a routine. First, he (nodding towards the teacher preparing papers at a desk) gives us notes from a PowerPoint for like, 20 minutes. Then, we read the same information from the textbook. If there is time left in class, he tries to get a discussion going which usually consists of the same two people answering dumb questions. The bell rings and we leave." The student shrugs his shoulders. "I like history but we never really talk to each other about the stuff we are learning." With a sigh, he turned back to the front and got ready to take notes.

Why Is This Item on the List So Important?

I read a quote recently on Twitter that went something like this: "Direct instruction did not get a bad reputation because it is a bad strategy. [It] got a bad reputation when it became our only strategy (Ward, 2018)." This really resonated with me. So many content area teachers I talk with say they would like to reach outside the box for learning strategies but the lack of time to cover content, and a distrust that students will learn something on their own, meant that using "notes," like those described by the student above, is a primary way most teachers deliver information. And while direct instruction has its place, we can't deny that it is discussion and discovery that really make learning enjoyable.

In a meeting with a group of high school science and social studies teachers I was working with, the principal made this bold statement: "If kids aren't leaving your class buzzing with a new and interesting piece of information, then you are teaching all wrong. Science and social studies should be the coolest part of their day." The strategies presented in this chapter will hopefully bring that "buzz" to your classroom.

> **"Do this, not that" principle #3:** DO Use small group reading and learning strategies to bring personal response and accountability to the content. DON'T make all reading and learning opportunities whole class.

To Get Started

To embrace small group learning strategies, the teacher has to move to the side and accept the role as facilitator. Starting way back with John Dewey and moving forward with Vygotsky, we have lots of research that supports the idea of the teacher as the "guide on the side" and not just the authority at the front of the room (King, 1993). Yet, teachers often resist the notion of stepping aside to let students learn in small groups for the following reasons (all gathered from a professional development session I conducted with science, social studies, health, and fine arts teachers in grades 3–12):

1. "I have too much to teach and not enough time."
2. "If I am not on top of the students, they do not learn anything."
3. "I tried some small group stuff once and it totally bombed."
4. "I spent so much time setting it up. It took forever to get to my actual content."

Let's debunk each one of these myths:

> *"I have too much to teach and not enough time."* Nope, I can't manufacture time for you. But what I can tell you is that if you give students finite, concrete blocks of time to accomplish something, they are

more likely to actually get it done than if you give long stretches with no real end point. There is something about setting a timer that lights a fire under their backsides to work. And if you build this into your classroom routines with small groups, they get used to working in a timely manner (Garrett, 2008).

"If I am not on top of the students, they do not learn anything." Nothing like small group work for social time! Let's just say this right out: YES, students are going to chat about things other than the content when they work in small groups—it's human nature to socialize! Think about your last staff or department meeting—was it on topic 100% of the time? We have to accept the social beings sitting in front of us as such and move past it. If we guide the students into the group work with clear expectations, start and stop times, and realistic outcomes, they will still learn (Cohen & Lotan, 2014).

"I tried some small group stuff once and it totally bombed." The key word in this quote? ONCE. If students are not used to small group work and instructional routines, then they must be modeled, tried, and adjusted until they fit. If your students do catch on in one go around, please email me and let me know because I want to observe your special, Stepford students.

"I spent so much time setting it up. It took forever to get to my actual content." This is an interesting one. The teacher felt that in the process of guiding pedagogy, she was losing content. Yet in the process of modeling and setting up small group learning opportunities, she was using her content in multiple ways. Together, we looked at her materials to ensure she was still meeting her standards prior to the full implementation of the strategy (which we will discuss below during the strategy updates).

Instructional Practices to Update

Updated Strategy #1: Apply Textmasters to Any Text to Facilitate Small Group Reading and Discussion

I first wrote about Textmasters in 2009. I created it in response to an English-turned-science teacher who wanted to bring the fun of literature circles to her science textbook (Wilfong, 2009). I updated the strategy again a few years later thinking specifically about science content (Wilfong, 2012).

The thinking behind literature circles matches perfectly with the goal of moving the teacher into a facilitator role:

♦ Students select or are assigned a text to read in a small group (four to six per group).

♦ Students pace the reading as a group based on a meeting schedule set by the teacher.

♦ Students read and respond to the text through a lens that differs from their other group members (summarizer, discussion director, word master, etc.), called roles.

♦ Students share their responses to the reading in their small group through that lens or role.

♦ Students prepare a brief presentation of the material for the rest of the class at the end of the entire text.

(Daniels, 1994)

In literature circles, each group reads a different novel. The presentations serve as a commercial for the book, tempting other students to want to read it next.

To adapt this strategy for the textbook, I first took a look at the role sheets. After consulting with a variety of content area teachers, we decided the goal would be for students to perform basic comprehension strategies: ask and answer questions about the text (Discussion Director), summarize the text (Summarizer), highlight key vocabulary (Vocabulary Enricher), and create a graphic organizer for the information presented in the text (Webmaster) (Wilfong, 2009). Later, we added a fifth role that concentrated on information from other content areas; e.g. if the text being read was from social studies, they would look for information regarding math and science (Content Catcher) (Wilfong, 2012). Figure 3.1 contains descriptions for each of the Textmaster roles. Blank templates for each role sheet are presented at the end of the chapter.

To train the students, I recommend tackling one role sheet a day. Read an article or textbook excerpt relating to the curriculum being studied, break it down using the role sheet, and then have students share in partners. Eventually, divide the students into groups, allow them to select their roles, read, complete the role sheets, and discuss.

The material used is up to the classroom teacher. This is a great way to bring a change in the routine to using the textbook; everyone reads the same section but discusses it in their Textmasters group. However, this is also a fantastic way to use a variety of articles at different levels that all address the same topic. Websites like Newslela, Digital Readworks, and Tween

Figure 3.1   Role Sheet Descriptors

Discussion Director
Your job is to develop a list of questions that your group might want to discuss about this part of the book. Don't worry about the small details; your task is to help people talk about the big ideas in the reading and share their reactions. Usually the best discussion questions come from your own thoughts, feelings, and concerns as you read.
Summarizer
Your job is to prepare a brief summary of today's reading. Your group discussion will start with your 1–2-minute statement that covers the key points, main highlights, and general idea of today's reading assignment.
Vocabulary Enricher
Your job is to be on the lookout for a few especially important words in today's reading. If you find words that are puzzling or unfamiliar, mark them while you are reading and then later jot down their definition, either from a dictionary or from some other source.
Webmaster
Your job is to take all the information that you have read and make a graphic organizer to show your understanding. Use keywords, phrases, and examples from your reading to make your organizer. You can use any type of graphic organizer you would like—i.e., web, pyramid, chart, etc.
Content Catcher
Your job is to read the text like a detective from another subject. Write down the information that you see to share with your group. Only fill out the section that relates to the text you are reading: SCIENCE or SOCIAL STUDIES

Tribune all have articles on a variety of topics presented at multiple levels. For example, everyone could be reading about erosion, but could be doing it at different levels. Similarly, groups of students could be reading on a similar topic, but using different articles, perhaps located in different geographic regions (e.g. erosion in Hawaii, erosion in Greenland, or erosion in Egypt). Finally, students could complete Textmasters on a variety of nonfiction books that follow a similar theme or idea. A colleague of mine recently shared about doing a round of Textmasters focusing on the United States presidents—each group chose a memoir of a recent president and read it, Textmasters-style.

In addition to training students through modeling the use of the role sheets and selecting the reading materials, the teacher helps students pace their reading. The number of days that will be devoted to Textmasters reading, completion of the role sheet, and discussion needs to be decided. Once these dates are calendared out, groups can meet and divide up the reading and role sheet responsibility (conveniently done for them on the Textmasters schedule; a sample schedule is included in Figure 3.2). A blank Textmasters schedule is presented at the end of the chapter.

Daily Schedule. On the days when Textmasters is in use, the use of a routine is helpful. I found in many classes that reading time needs to be provided in class so that it actually gets done. Time for reading, role completion, and then discussion should all be included within a single day, when possible.

Figure 3.2 Sample Textmasters Schedule for Students

Textmasters Schedule

*Decide which group member will be A, B, C, D, and E (if necessary). Record that below. Then, read the schedule to see which role you will have each time we meet. If you only have four people in your group, there will not be a Member E.

Member A-___Macy Allen_____
Member B-_____Hollyann Mullett_____
Member C-_____Blaise Kessler_____
Member D-_____
Member E-_____

Meetings:	Discussion Director	Vocabulary Enricher	Summarizer	Webmaster
Meeting 1 Date: 3/12 Chapter 1	A/E	B	C	D
Meeting 2 Date: 3/19 Chapters 2	D	A/E	B	C
Meeting 3 Date: 4/2 Chapter 3	C	D	A/E	B
Meeting 4 Date: 4/9 Chapters 4 and 5	B	C	D	A/E

The teacher who piloted this strategy reported that her organizational skills were called to use here: She created a folder for each student that contained their Textmasters schedule and all necessary role sheets (Wilfong, 2009). A few years later, someone else updated this process from folders to computers. This teacher used her Google Classroom to do the same thing—every student had a folder with a Google Doc for the schedule of the text they were reading and links to the role sheets for completion. Figure 3.3 includes a suggested routine for a Textmasters day.

Times can be adjusted based on the amount of reading you are having students complete, the kinds of discussion taking place, and whether you are having students create some kind of a culminating activity or presentation.

Speaking of which . . . to end Textmasters, rather than a commercial, like is commonly used with literature circles, many teachers have students create some sort of a presentation to review material learned. This is especially helpful when all students are reading and discussing the same topic, whether through the textbook or different materials. Each group selects a different presentation mode and the teacher extends the discussion time to include a work session on the culminating activity. These presentations can serve as a review for an assessment or paper and are way more effective than a study guide.

I was recently in a seventh-grade social studies class that was studying world religions. Textmasters was done using the textbook, so all students had read and discussed the same material. On the presentation day, students heard the same information, but in eight different ways through the eight different presentations. These were everything from a Jeopardy game, a Readers' Theatre, a newscast, and an interactive Prezi. A test followed the presentations and the teacher was thrilled to see how this type of review paid off, versus the typical study guide she would normally hand out.

Since the creation of the strategy, Harvey Daniels, the originator of literature circles, has updated his own strategy by eliminating role sheets. He saw too many instances of students simply reading from their role sheets and not delving into true discussion. He encouraged teachers to let go of

Figure 3.3 Suggested Textmasters Routine

2 minutes – Find materials and settle in for reading
15 minutes – Reading and role sheet completion
10 minutes – Share role sheets with group members; discussion
5 minutes – Reflection; exit ticket

Figure 3.4 Social Studies Specific Roles

Geographer
Your job is to read the text with the lens of a geographer. How does the location of what happened in the text impact the events? Why is the geography of what takes place in the text important?
Economist
Your job is to read the text from an Economist's point of view – how does money impact this text?
Historian
Your job is to document the impact of historical events on the text read. What came before? What came afterwards? What is the importance of these events?
Politician
Your job is to view the text from the lens of a government official. What is the impact of the role of government in the text?

the role sheets and instead come to discussion with a sticky note or reflection (Daniels & Harvey, 2015). In my own experience, starting with the role sheets and then removing them as students become comfortable with the strategy seems to work best; however, I have found that students like having the "lens" through which to view the material.

Social Studies Specific Textmasters. A few years after I first wrote about Textmasters, a middle school social studies teacher challenged me to think about content-specific roles. The National Council of Social Studies had just released their own "lenses" through which to view social studies material and they were easily adapted into new, social studies specific, role sheets. Figure 3.4 presents the social studies specific roles. The full roles are included at the end of the chapter.

Updated Strategy #2: Bringing S.O.L.E. into the Classroom

Ready to really think outside the box? Then S.O.L.E., or Student Organized Learning Environments, might be for you. S.O.L.E. was first introduced by Sugata Mitra as a way to bring learning to students, even in the most remote locations, by posing "big questions" for students to inquire and present

Figure 3.5 Sample Big Questions

What is a brain? How and why do landforms change over time? Can we live on a different planet? Why do elephants have long trunks? What is freedom? Why do people follow religions? What is the purpose of art? Why do humans like music? What is a fair price for a product? When did time begin? How should we address climate change? Is war necessary?

findings (School in the Cloud, 2018). Students are encouraged to research, collaborate, and critically think about their answers to the "big question" before presenting their information in a meaningful and engaging way. When Mitra presented his research on the impact this type of learning had on students, educators from traditional classrooms reacted in a big way—could something like this work in a regular ol' classroom?

Here is how S.O.L.E. could work in your classroom:

1. Asking the Big Question. Finding a question to investigate is key. Questions can be about anything but what they can't be is answered in a single word, nor can there really be one "right" answer. Figure 3.5 shares some innovative Big Questions from a variety of sources that will meet the needs of different content areas.

2. Time to investigate! Students are given a short period (40 minutes or so) to respond to the question in groups of four. Each group needs access to at least one computer. During investigation, students are allowed to ask you questions and ask other groups questions. Having one student as the liason to other groups and the teacher might be helpful. As students begin to gather their information, they organize it into a presentable format—PowerPoint, Prezi, video, etc.

3. Review answers to the Big Question. Students give their brief presentations and discussion is held over the variety of responses.

S.O.L.E. is not intended to be used every day but is a great way to change up learning and research in any classroom once a week, once a month, or once a quarter.

My own skepticism of S.O.L.E. in real classrooms was deep until I met a seventh-grade social studies teacher, Dan Juliani, who waxed poetic about the impact on the use of S.O.L.E. with his students. Here is how he made it work in his room:

> I was nervous to implement it because of the common problems we see with group work (i.e. students not doing equal work,

fooling around, plagiarism, etc.) but the way I incorporated it was to give students their groups the day before and have them fill out a duties list so that each student was responsible for some aspect of the work (research, note taking, creating a poster or Google slides, and presenting). Students also assessed group members on how well they worked. Each group of three to four students would have one Chromebook provided to them, but they were also free to use their own devices as well. What worried me initially is that students would be off-task, but given that they had to complete and present their research in one period and that their peers were grading them, off-task behavior was minimal. I included a S.O.L.E. in each unit we covered in World History and it was a great tool to not only use to introduce a new unit (i.e. "What was the Renaissance?"), but to get students to research a topic we were covering in class with more depth. For instance, when we were discussing Ancient Rome and Christianity, the students completed a S.O.L.E. that asked them "What caused Christianity to spread so quickly?" In every class, most groups had different reasons and evidence to why they felt it spread. While I was planning to move on to the next section, I decided to spend the next few days and use student findings to have discussions and debates about the different reasons and which may have been more important. The questions are very open and allow students to come up with different answers and responses. Students would then present their findings with either a poster, Google Slides, or a skit.

Dan encourages teachers to display a timer on the board so students use time effectively and to give real-time feedback during the investigation period so that students see how to research and work successfully.

In an era of fake news, students more than ever need to be thinking about who is presenting information, how it is presented, and truly thinking about the differences between facts and opinions (Beers and Probst, 2017). S.O.L.E. really encourages students to think about their resources, reach beyond Wikipedia and look at articles, visuals, and more to find an appropriate response to the Big Question. In the one S.O.L.E. session I observed, students discussed authors' point of view and bias, separated facts from opinions, and sought out primary and secondary sources to make points. All this was done without intervention from the teacher—it was impressive! The other piece that impressed me so much about S.O.L.E. was the fact that students were writing—argumentative texts, informative texts, or narrative texts, depending on the question—without a single complaint. The authentic nature of the research and the text encouraged writing in the most natural of ways.

There are two major resources on the internet to help support teachers in their implementation of S.O.L.E:

1. School in the Cloud: www.theschoolinthecloud.org

2. Start S.O.L.E: https://startsole.org

Common Core Connection

The strategies in this chapter support several of the Common Core State Standards for Literacy in History/Social Studies, Science, & Technical Subjects:

Reading Standards (History/Social Studies)

6–8	9–10	11–12
6–8.1 Cite specific textual evidence to support analysis of primary and secondary sources. 6–8.2 Determine the central ideas or information of a primary or secondary source; provide an accurate summary of the source distinct from prior knowledge or opinions. 6–8.3 Identify key steps in a text's description of a process related to history/social studies (e.g., how a bill becomes law, how interest rates are raised or lowered).	9–10.1 Cite specific textual evidence to support analysis of primary and secondary sources, attending to such features as the date and origin of the information. 9–10.2 Determine the central ideas or information of a primary or secondary source; provide an accurate summary of how key events or ideas develop over the course of the text. 9–10.3 Analyze in detail a series of events described in a text; determine whether earlier events caused later ones or simply preceded them.	11–12.1 Cite specific textual evidence to support analysis of primary and secondary sources, connecting insights gained from specific details to an understanding of the text as a whole. 11–12.2 Determine the central ideas or information of a primary or secondary source; provide an accurate summary that makes clear the relationships among the key details and ideas. 11–12.3 Evaluate various explanations for actions or events and determine which explanation best accords with textual evidence, acknowledging where the text leaves matters uncertain.

(Continued)

(Continued)

6–8	9–10	11–12
6–8.4 Determine the meaning of words and phrases as they are used in a text, including vocabulary specific to domains related to history/social studies.	9–10.4 Determine the meaning of words and phrases as they are used in a text, including vocabulary describing political, social, or economic aspects of history/social science.	11–12.4 Determine the meaning of words and phrases as they are used in a text, including analyzing how an author uses and refines the meaning of a key term over the course of a text (e.g., how Madison defines *faction* in *Federalist* No. 10).
6–8.6 Identify aspects of a text that reveal an author's point of view or purpose (e.g., loaded language, inclusion or avoidance of particular facts).	9–10.6 Compare the point of view of two or more authors for how they treat the same or similar topics, including which details they include and emphasize in their respective accounts.	11–12.6 Evaluate authors' differing points of view on the same historical event or issue by assessing the authors' claims, reasoning, and evidence.
6–8.7 Integrate visual information (e.g., in charts, graphs, photographs, videos, or maps) with other information in print and digital texts.	9–10.7 Integrate quantitative or technical analysis (e.g., charts, research data) with qualitative analysis in print or digital text.	11–12.7 Integrate and evaluate multiple sources of information presented in diverse formats and media (e.g., visually, quantitatively, as well as in words) in order to address a question or solve a problem.
6–8.8 Distinguish among fact, opinion, and reasoned judgment in a text.	9–10.8 Assess the extent to which the reasoning and evidence in a text support the author's claims.	11–12.8 Evaluate an author's premises, claims, and evidence by corroborating or challenging them with other information.
6–8.9 Analyze the relationship between a primary and secondary source on the same topic.	9–10.9 Compare and contrast treatments of the same topic in several primary and secondary sources.	11–12.9 Integrate information from diverse sources, both primary and secondary, into a coherent understanding of an idea or event, noting discrepancies among sources.
6–8.10 By the end of grade 8, read and comprehend history/ social studies texts in the grades 6–8 text complexity band independently and proficiently.	9–10.10 By the end of grade 10, read and comprehend history/ social studies texts in the grades 9–10 text complexity band independently and proficiently.	11–12.10 By the end of grade 12, read and compre-hend history/social studies texts in the grades 11-CCR text complexity band inde-pendently and proficiently.

Reading Standards (Science & Technical Subjects)

6–8	9–10	11–12
6–8.1 Cite specific textual evidence to support analysis of science and technical texts.	9–10.1 Cite specific textual evidence to support analysis of science and technical texts, attending to the precise details of explanations or descriptions.	11–12.1 Cite specific textual evidence to support analysis of science and technical texts, attending to important distinctions the author makes and to any gaps or inconsistencies in the account.
6–8.2 Determine the central ideas or conclusions of a text; provide an accurate summary of the text distinct from prior knowledge or opinions.	9–10.2 Determine the central ideas or conclusions of a text; trace the text's explanation or depiction of a complex process, phenomenon, or concept; provide an accurate summary of the text.	11–12.2 Determine the central ideas or conclusions of a text; summarize complex concepts, processes, or information presented in a text by paraphrasing them in simpler but still accurate terms.
6–8.4 Determine the meaning of symbols, key terms, and other domain-specific words and phrases as they are used in a specific scientific or technical context relevant to *grades 6–8 texts and topics*.	9–10.4 Determine the meaning of symbols, key terms, and other domain-specific words and phrases as they are used in a specific scientific or technical context relevant to *grades 9–10 texts and topics*.	11–12.4 Determine the meaning of symbols, key terms, and other domain-specific words and phrases as they are used in a specific scientific or technical context relevant to *grades 11–12 texts and topics*.
6–8.6 Analyze the author's purpose in providing an explanation, describing a procedure, or discussing an experiment in a text.	9–10.6 Analyze the author's purpose in providing an explanation, describing a procedure, or discussing an experiment in a text, defining the question the author seeks to address.	11–12.6 Analyze the author's purpose in providing an explanation, describing a procedure, or discussing an experiment in a text, identifying important issues that remain unresolved.
6–8.7 Integrate quantitative or technical information expressed in words in a text with a version of that information expressed visually (e.g., in a flowchart, diagram, model, graph, or table).	9–10.8 Assess the extent to which the reasoning and evidence in a text support the	
6–8.8 Distinguish among facts, reasoned judgment based on		

(Continued)

(Continued)

6–8	9–10	11–12
research findings, and speculation in a text. 6–8.9 Compare and contrast the information gained from experiments, simulations, video, or multimedia sources with that gained from reading a text on the same topic. 6–8.10 By the end of grade 8, read and comprehend science/technical texts in the grades 6–8 text complexity band independently and proficiently.	author's claim or a recommendation for solving a scientific or technical problem. 9–10.9 Compare and contrast findings presented in a text to those from other sources (including their own experiments), noting when the findings support or contradict previous explanations or accounts. 9–10.10 By the end of grade 10, read and comprehend science/technical texts in the grades 9–10 text complexity band independently and proficiently.	11–12.7 Integrate and evaluate multiple sources of information presented in diverse formats and media (e.g., quantitative data, video, multimedia) in order to address a question or solve a problem. 11–12.8 Evaluate the hypotheses, data, analysis, and conclusions in a science or technical text, verifying the data when possible and corroborating or challenging conclusions with other sources of information. 11–12.9 Synthesize information from a range of sources (e.g., texts, experiments, simulations) into a coherent understanding of a process, phenomenon, or concept, resolving conflicting information when possible. 11–12.10 By the end of grade 12, read and comprehend science/technical texts in the grades 11-CCR text complexity band independently and proficiently.

Writing Standards (History/Social Studies/Science/Other Technical Subjects)

6–8	9–10	11–12
6–8.1 Write arguments focused on *discipline-specific content*	9–10.1 Write arguments focused on *discipline-specific content*.	11–12.1 Write arguments focused on *discipline-specific content*.
6–8.1a Introduce claim(s) about a topic or issue, acknowledge and distinguish the claim(s) from alternate or opposing claims, and organize the reasons and evidence logically.	9–10.1a Introduce precise claim(s), distinguish the claim(s) from alternate or opposing claims, and create an organization that establishes clear relationships among the claim(s), counterclaims, reasons, and evidence.	11–12.1a Introduce precise, knowledgeable claim(s), establish the significance of the claim(s), distinguish the claim(s) from alternate or opposing claims, and create an organization that logically sequences the claim(s), counterclaims, reasons, and evidence.
6–8.1b Support claim(s) with logical reasoning and relevant, accurate data and evidence that demonstrate an understanding of the topic or text, using credible sources.	9–10.1b Develop claim(s) and counterclaims fairly, supplying data and evidence for each while pointing out the strengths and limitations of both claim(s) and counterclaims in a discipline-appropriate form and in a manner that anticipates the audience's knowledge level and concerns.	11–12.1b Develop claim(s) and counterclaims fairly and thoroughly, supplying the most relevant data and evidence for each while pointing out the strengths and limitations of both claim(s) and counterclaims in a discipline-appropriate form that anticipates the audience's knowledge level, concerns, values, and possible biases.
6–8.1c Use words, phrases, and clauses to create cohesion and clarify the relationships among claim(s), counterclaims, reasons, and evidence.	9–10.1c Use words, phrases, and clauses to link the major sections of the text, create cohesion, and clarify the relationships between claim(s) and reasons, between reasons and evidence, and between claim(s) and counterclaims.	11–12.1c Use words, phrases, and clauses as well as varied syntax to link the major sections of the text, create cohesion, and clarify the relationships
6–8.1d Establish and maintain a formal style.		
6–8.1e Provide a concluding statement or section that follows from and supports the argument presented.		
6–8.2 Write informative/ explanatory texts, including the narration of historical events, scientific procedures/		

(*Continued*)

6–8	9–10	11–12
experiments, or technical processes. 6–8.2a Introduce a topic clearly, previewing what is to follow; organize ideas, concepts, and information into broader categories as appropriate to achieving purpose; include formatting (e.g., headings), graphics (e.g., charts, tables), and multimedia when useful to aiding comprehension. 6–8.2b Develop the topic with relevant, well-chosen facts, definitions, concrete details, quotations, or other information and examples. 6–8.2c Use appropriate and varied transitions to create cohesion and clarify the relationships among ideas and concepts. 6–8.2d Use precise language and domain-specific vocabulary to inform about or explain the topic. 6–8.2e Establish and maintain a formal style and objective tone. 6–8.2f Provide a concluding statement or section that follows from and supports	9–10.1d Establish and maintain a formal style and objective tone while attending to the norms and conventions of the discipline in which they are writing. 9–10.1e Provide a concluding statement or section that follows from or supports the argument presented. 9–10.2 Write informative/explanatory texts, including the narration of historical events, scientific procedures/experiments, or technical processes. 9–10.2a Introduce a topic and organize ideas, concepts, and information to make important connections and distinctions; include formatting (e.g., headings), graphics (e.g., figures, tables), and multimedia when useful to aiding comprehension. 9–10.2b Develop the topic with well-chosen, relevant, and sufficient facts, extended definitions, concrete details, quotations, or other information and examples appropriate to the audience's knowledge of the topic.	between claim(s) and reasons, between reasons and evidence, and between claim(s) and counterclaims. 11–12.1d Establish and maintain a formal style and objective tone while attending to the norms and conventions of the discipline in which they are writing. 11–12.1e Provide a concluding statement or section that follows from or supports the argument presented. 11–12.2 Write informative/explanatory texts, including the narration of historical events, scientific procedures/experiments, or technical processes. 11–12.2a Introduce a topic and organize complex ideas, concepts, and information so that each new element builds on that which precedes it to create a unified whole; include formatting (e.g., headings), graphics (e.g., figures, tables), and multimedia when useful to aiding comprehension. 11–12.2b Develop the topic thoroughly

6–8	9–10	11–12
the information or explanation presented. 6–8.4 Produce clear and coherent writing in which the development, organization, and style are appropriate to task, purpose, and audience. 6–8.5 With some guidance and support from peers and adults, develop and strengthen writing as needed by planning, revising, editing, rewriting, or trying a new approach, focusing on how well purpose and audience have been addressed. 6–8.6 Use technology, including the Internet, to produce and publish writing and present the relationships between information and ideas clearly and efficiently. 6–8.7 Conduct short research projects to answer a question (including a self-generated question), drawing on several sources and generating additional related, focused questions that allow for multiple avenues of exploration. 6–8.8 Gather relevant information from multiple print and digital sources,	9–10.2c Use varied transitions and sentence structures to link the major sections of the text, create cohesion, and clarify the relationships among ideas and concepts. 9–10.2d Use precise language and domain-specific vocabulary to manage the complexity of the topic and convey a style appropriate to the discipline and context as well as to the expertise of likely readers. 9–10.2e Establish and maintain a formal style and objective tone while attending to the norms and conventions of the discipline in which they are writing. 9–10.2f Provide a concluding statement or section that follows from and supports the information or explanation presented (e.g., articulating implications or the significance of the topic). 9–10.4 Produce clear and coherent writing in which the development, organization, and style are appropriate to task, purpose, and audience.	by selecting the most significant and relevant facts, extended definitions, concrete details, quotations, or other information and examples appropriate to the audience's knowledge of the topic. 11–12.2c Use varied transitions and sentence structures to link the major sections of the text, create cohesion, and clarify the relationships among complex ideas and concepts. 11–12.2d Use precise language, domain-specific vocabulary and techniques such as metaphor, simile, and analogy to manage the complexity of the topic; convey a knowledgeable stance in a style that responds to the discipline and context as well as to the expertise of likely readers. 11–12.2e Provide a concluding statement or section that follows from and supports the information or explanation provided (e.g., articulating implications or the significance of the topic).

(Continued)

(Continued)

6–8	9–10	11–12
using search terms effectively; assess the credibility and accuracy of each source; and quote or paraphrase the data and conclusions of others while avoiding plagiarism and following a standard format for citations. 6–8.9 Draw evidence from informational texts to support analysis, reflection, and research. 6–8.10 Write routinely over extended time frames (time for reflection and revision) and shorter time frames (a single sitting or a day or two) for a range of discipline-specific tasks, purposes, and audiences.	9–10.5 Develop and strengthen writing as needed by planning, revising, editing, rewriting, or trying a new approach, focusing on addressing what is most significant for a specific purpose and audience. 9–10.6 Use technology, including the Internet, to produce, publish, and update individual or shared writing products, taking advantage of technology's capacity to link to other information and to display information flexibly and dynamically. 9–10.7 Conduct short as well as more sustained research projects to answer a question (including a self-generated question) or solve a problem; narrow or broaden the inquiry when appropriate; synthesize multiple sources on the subject, demonstrating understanding of the subject under investigation.	11–12.4 Produce clear and coherent writing in which the development, organization, and style are appropriate to task, purpose, and audience. 11–12.5 Develop and strengthen writing as needed by planning, revising, editing, rewriting, or trying a new approach, focusing on addressing what is most significant for a specific purpose and audience. 11–12.6 Use technology, including the Internet, to produce, publish, and update individual or shared writing products in response to ongoing feedback, including new arguments or information. 11–12.7 Conduct short as well as more sustained research projects to answer a question (including a self-generated question) or solve a problem; narrow or broaden the inquiry when appropriate; synthesize multiple sources on the subject, demonstrating understanding of the subject under investigation.

6–8	9–10	11–12
	9–10.8 Gather relevant information from multiple authoritative print and digital sources, using advanced searches effectively; assess the usefulness of each source in answering the research question; integrate information into the text selectively to maintain the flow of ideas, avoiding plagiarism and following a standard format for citation. 9–10.9 Draw evidence from informational texts to support analysis, reflection, and research. 9–10.10 Write routinely over extended time frames (time for reflection and revision) and shorter time frames (a single sitting or a day or two) for a range of discipline-specific tasks, purposes, and audiences.	11–12.8 Gather relevant information from multiple authoritative print and digital sources, using advanced searches effectively; assess the strengths and limitations of each source in terms of the specific task, purpose, and audience; integrate information into the text selectively to maintain the flow of ideas, avoiding plagiarism and overreliance on any one source and following a standard format for citation. 11–12.9 Draw evidence from informational texts to support analysis, reflection, and research. 11–12.10 Write routinely over extended time frames (time for reflection and revision) and shorter time frames (a single sitting or a day or two) for a range of discipline-specific tasks, purposes, and audiences.

Action Steps

Becoming a guide on the side isn't easy—but it is worth it in the long run! It's time to take some action . . .

1) Which version of Textmasters would work best for your classroom—the generic (most comprehension-focused) version or a more specific, content-based version? Why?

   _____

   _____

   _____

2) Social studies has it made with the content-based version of Textmasters. If you are a teacher of another content area, what are some roles you could brainstorm to create your own, content-based versions of the role sheets?

   _____

   _____

   _____

3) What kinds of texts appeal most to you when implementing Textmasters: the textbook, articles, a variety of nonfiction or fiction books, or something else? Why?

   _____

   _____

   _____

4) Could you see yourself using S.O.LE.? Why or why not?

   _____

   _____

   _____

5) Brainstorm three Big Questions you could use over the course of a school year in a S.O.L.E. in your classroom:

   a.

   b.

   c.

Works Cited

Beers, K., & Probst, R. (2017). *Disrupting thinking: Why how we read matters.* New York, NY: Scholastic.

Cohen, E., & Lotan, R. (2014). *Designing groupwork: Strategies for the heterogenous classroom* (3rd ed.). New York, NY: Teachers College Press.

Daniels, H. (1994). *Literature circles: Voice and choice in book clubs and reading groups.* Portland, ME: Stenhouse.

Daniels, H., & Harvey, S. (2015). *Comprehension and collaboration, revised.* Portsmouth, NH: Heinemann.

Garrett, T. (2008). Student-centered and teacher-centered classroom management: A case study of three elementary teachers. *The Journal of Classroom Interaction, 43,* 34–47.

King, A. (1993). From sage on the stage to guide on the side. *College Teaching, 41,* 30–35.

School in the Cloud. (n.d.). Retrieved July 24, 2018, from www.theschoolinthecloud. org/

Start S.O.L.E. (n.d.). Retrieved July 24, 2018, from https://startsole.org

Ward, P. [MfcsdCurriculum]. (2018, June 29). "Direct Instruction isn't a bad method of teaching, but as educators, we gave it a bad name when it became our ONLY . . . https://t.co/qmhy5z7OZS [Tweet]. Retrieved from https://twitter.com/ MfcsdCurriculum/status/1012702798239023104

Wilfong, L. G. (2009). Textmasters: Bringing literature circles to textbook reading across the curriculum. *Journal of Adolescent and Adult Literacy, 53,* 164–171.

Wilfong, L. G. (2012). The science text for all: Using Textmaster to help all students access written science content. *Science Scope, 35,* 46–53.

<u>Textmasters Role Sheet—Summarizer</u>

Meeting Date: _____ Assignment Pages: _____ to _____

Summarizer: Your job is to prepare a brief summary of today's reading. Your group discussion will start with your 1–2 minute statement that covers the key points, main highlights, and general idea of today's reading assignment.

Key Points:

1. _____

2. _____

3. _____

4. _____

Summary:

_____

_____

_____

_____

_____

_____

Name: _____

Textmasters Role
Sheet—Discussion Director

Meeting Date: _____ Assignment Pages: _____ to _____

Discussion Director: Your job is to develop a list of questions that your group might want to discuss about this part of the book. Don't worry about the small details; your task is to help people talk over the big ideas in the reading and share their reactions. Usually the best discussion questions come from your own thoughts, feelings, and concerns as you read. You can list them below during or after your reading. You may also use some of the general questions below to develop topics for your group.

Possible Discussion Questions or Topics:

1. _____

2. _____

3. _____

4. _____

Sample questions

- ♦ Did today's reading remind you of any real-life experiences?
- ♦ What questions did you have when you finished this section?
- ♦ Did anything in this section of the book surprise you?
- ♦ What are some things you think will be talked about next?

Connections:

Text to Text: _____

Text to Self: _____

Text to World: _____

* Adapted from Daniels, H. (1994). *Literature circles: Voice and choice in the student-centered classroom.* York, ME: Stenhouse Pub.

Textmasters Role Sheet—Vocabulary Enricher

Meeting Date: _____ Assignment Pages: _____ to _____

Vocabulary Enricher: Your job is to be on the lookout for a few especially important words in today's reading. If you find words that are puzzling or unfamiliar, mark them while you are reading and then later jot down their definition, either from a dictionary or from some other source. You may also run across familiar words that stand out somehow in the reading— words that are repeated a lot, are used in an unusual way, or provide a key to the meaning of the text. Mark these special words, and be ready to point them out to the group. When your circle meets, help members find and discuss these words.

Page #	Word	Meaning	Example	Sketch

Textmasters Role Sheet—Webmaster

Meeting Date: _____ Assignment Pages: _____ to _____

Webmaster: Your job is to take all the information that you have read
and make a graphic organizer to show your understanding. Use key words,
phrases, and examples from your reading to make your organizer. You can use
any type of graphic organizer you would like—i.e. web, pyramid, chart, etc.

Name: _____

Textmasters Role Sheet—Content Catcher

Meeting Date: _____ Assignment Pages: _____ to _____

Content Catcher: Your job is to read the text like a detective from another subject. Write down the information that you see to share with your group. Only fill out the section that relates to the text you are reading: SCIENCE or SOCIAL STUDIES.

If this is a SCIENCE text, you are looking for math and social studies ideas:

Math ideas

1. _____
   _____
2. _____
   _____

Social studies ideas

1. _____
   _____
2. _____
   _____

If this is a SOCIAL STUDIES text, you are looking for science and math ideas:

Math ideas

1. _____
   _____
2. _____
   _____

Science ideas

1. _____
   _____
2. _____
   _____

Textmasters Schedule

*Decide which group member will be A, B, C, D, and E (if necessary). Record that below. Then, read the schedule to see which role you will have each time we meet. If you only have four people in your group, there will not be a Member E.

Member A-___ _____

Member B-_____ _____

Member C-_____ _____

Member D-_____

Member E-_____

Meetings:	Discussion Director	Vocabulary Enricher	Summarizer	Webmaster
Meeting 1 Date: Pages to be read:	A/E	B	C	D
Meeting 2 Date: Pages to be read:	D	A/E	B	C
Meeting 3 Date: Pages to be read:	C	D	A/E	B
Meeting 4 Date: Pages to be read:	B	C	D	A/E

Name: _____

Social Studies Textmasters
Role Sheet—Geographer

Meeting Date: _____ Assignment Pages: _____ to _____

Geographer: Your job is to read the text with the lens of a geographer. How does the location of what happened in the text impact the events? Why is the geography of what takes place in the text important?

Identify up to three physical features of the location described in the text. List them here:

1. _____

2. _____

3. _____

Choose one of the questions below and answer it with the lens of a geographer:

a) How do these physical features impact the events in the text?

b) How were there negative or positive consequences on the environment?

c) How has the location influenced the movement of people, ideas, and products?

d) How did the region described develop and/or change?

_____

_____

_____

_____

_____

Select one of the physical features listed above. Define and sketch the word.

Word	Define	Sketch

Name: _____

Social Studies Textmasters
Role Sheet—Economist

Meeting Date: _____ Assignment Pages: _____ to _____

Economist: Your job is to read the text from an economist's point of view—how does money impact this text?

List up to three ways money/goods/services are either spent or earned in this text:

1. _____

2. _____

3. _____

Choose one of the questions below and answer it with the lens of an economist:

a) What decisions were made about spending money in this text?
b) In what order were economic decisions made in this text?
c) Who was impacted by the economic decisions in this text?

_____

_____

_____

_____

_____   _____

Select one of the productive resources in the text. Define and sketch the word.

Word	Define	Sketch

 Name: _____

<u>Social Studies Textmasters</u>
<u>Role Sheet—Historian</u>

Meeting Date: _____ Assignment Pages: _____ to _____

Historian: Your job is to document the impact of historical events on the text read. What came before? What came afterwards? What is the importance of these events?

What are two actions that preceded the events described in the text?

1. _____

_____

2. _____

_____

Predict two actions that came after the events described in the text?

1. _____

_____

2. _____

_____

What are two reasons the events described in the text are important?

1. _____

_____

2. _____

_____

Connection/Question: List either one connection or one question you have related to the events of the text.

_____

_____

_____

_____

_____

Textmasters Role Sheet—Politician

Meeting Date: _____ Assignment Pages: _____ to _____

Policitian: Your job is to view the text from the lens of a government official. What is the impact of the role of government in the text?

List three ways that government played a role in the text:

1. _____

_____

2. _____

_____

3. _____

_____

Choose one of the questions below and answer it with the lens of a political scientist:

a) What would have been the consequences had there been no government involved in the events in the text?
b) Describe how was the government helpful in this text?
c) Or, describe how the government was not helpful in this text?

_____

_____

_____

_____

_____

_____

Identify one word in the text related to government. Define and sketch the word.

Word	Define	Sketch

Chapter 4

Address Discipline-Specific Content Reading Strategies

A sixth-grade teaching team, consisting of teachers from the four major content areas, share students and have invited me to sit in on a team meeting as they look at the workload they will be assigning students over the course of a quarter. Each had brought their curriculum map. They started by examining the amount of reading they would be assigning in class. The language arts teacher talked about the independent reading her students would be doing while the social studies teacher laid out a series of articles looking at various civilizations. When it was her turn, the science teacher shrugged her shoulders, "We won't be doing a ton of reading. There is a big experiment coming up so we will be preparing for that." "There isn't reading that goes with that, you know, to prepare for the experiment?" I asked. She shook her head. We all turned to the math teacher, who laughed. "I teach math," she explained. "There is not a bunch of reading."

Why Is This Item on the List So Important?

The anecdote above was a perfect opportunity to grasp the different kinds of reading we do in different disciplines (and was actually one of the jumping-off points for this book!). When we pressed the science teacher, it turned out there was a ton of reading that the students would be doing in conjunction with the experiment: building background knowledge, following the steps of the experiment itself, and looking at models of write-ups before the students wrote their own. Even in math, where there is "not a bunch of reading," we saw that each of her lessons had a real-world application for students to read and discuss, along with an explanation for the multi-step problems they were working on. When we compiled all the reading that students would be doing in each content area that semester, we filled the teacher office we were sitting in with text of all shapes and sizes.

An outcome of this important conversation was the realization of how differently students were reading in each one of these classes. In language arts, the students were reading a text of their choice while applying an analysis standard. In social studies, students were comparing and contrasting two civilizations using a variety of sources. In science, students were preparing for an experiment by learning about the topic, following steps in a process, and then studying model write-ups. And in math, students were learning about real-world applications for the computations they were working on. At the end of this work session, we all agreed that our students were being flooded (in a good way!) with text, and the texts we were reading and how we needed to approach them were going to be very different.

> *"Do this, not that" principle #3: DO address discipline-specific content reading strategies. DON'T ignore the items that make reading in different disciplines unique.*

To Get Started

One of the most important things we can do as teachers of different disciplines is to make our purposes for reading clear. Many of our students might remember author's purpose from their earlier learning: Authors write to persuade, inform, or entertain (Cleaver, 2018). If students are entering our classrooms with this correct, but narrow, view of all texts, then reading in each of our content areas will also be narrow. Table 4.1 summarizes different ways of reading in each discipline and examples of specific texts that can be used to model this type of reading. To begin the year in each discipline, I recommend showing this chart to students along with models for each purpose to broaden their definition of reading and focus them on *how* and *why* we read in this particular class. Then, each time we tackle a text, we could hold a brief discussion on what our purpose is for reading this text in this discipline.

Table 4.1 Purposes for Reading Across the Disciplines

Content Area	Purpose for Reading	Sample Text
Social studies	*Sourcing*—Who created the text and how does that affect the viewpoint and reliability? *Corroborating*—Comparing and contrasting points of view across texts *Contextualizing*—Placing a document into historical context (date, place, events)	Primary documents Secondary documents Newspaper articles (both current and historical) Maps
Science	*Apply*—Learn about and use models and carry out investigations *Explore*—How the world works and connects, physically and biologically *Test*—See how hypotheses developed by others work out	Laboratory directions Charts and graphs Scientific journal articles
Math	*Critique*—Judge mathematical arguments	Charts and graphs Proofs
Language arts	*Author's Craft*—Analyze choices an author made while writing *Theme*—Exploring the human experience	Short stories Novels Op/Ed pieces Journal articles
Art/ Music	*Respond*—Aesthetically judge a piece *Critique*—Judge a piece in terms of technique or movement *Connect*—Draw connections between pieces among artists or musicians	Works of art Works of music

(Fisher & Frey, 2017; Johnson & Watson, 2011; Lapp, Grant, Moss, & Johnson, 2013; Siebert, et al., 2016)

Part of embracing discipline-specific reading is broadening our view of what constitutes a text. In my English teacher mind, a text is composed of words. But to a mathematician, a text can be a chart or graph. To an artist, it can be painting on a canvas or a sculpture. To a historian, a text might be a political cartoon or a map. A broader definition of text is inclusive to all of the disciplines (Smagorinsky, 2001). In addition, widening our definition of texts helps us as teachers move beyond the idea of memorizing "stuff" as learning and really thinking about what it means to interpret information in a variety of contexts (Moje, 2015).

Instructional Practices to Update

Updated Strategy #1: Comparing Multiple Texts Using an I-Chart (Cummins, 2017)

Having students research to learn in a content area can turn into an endless game of Googling/Wikipedia-ing (the latter verb I just invented). And in many cases, students will find one source and use it as *the* source; whether it is right or wrong, it holds the basic answers (they hope) they need to complete the assignment. An I-Chart can be a solution to the endless Googling. The purpose of an I-Chart is to narrow research based on specific questions while encouraging students to use multiple sources to answer these questions (Cummins, 2017).

While this strategy is perfect for the social studies purpose of reading to compare sources and corroborate, I originally read about it as a way to help facilitate research using multiple texts in a science classroom (Cummins, 2017). In fact, this strategy can be adjusted to fit the purposes for reading in all disciplines by simply changing out the questions to be answered. Table 4.2 presents a basic I-Chart (a full template is included at the end of the chapter).

Students can brainstorm their own questions and find their own resources but to really get at discipline-specific literacy, specific questions can be planted to ensure that students are reading like historians/geographers/politicans/scientists/artists/mathematicians/authors. Table 4.3 provides a list of such questions to ensure discipline-specific literacy is happening during this strategy.

Table 4.2 Basic I-Chart

Student Name	Question #1	Question #2	Question #3
What I already know about this topic			
Resource #1:			
Resource #2:			
Resource #3:			
Summary across resources:			

Table 4.3 Possible Discipline-Specific Questions to Use with the I-Chart

Content Area	Possible Questions
Social studies	◆ Who wrote the text? What are their qualifications? How reliable is this text? ◆ What is the viewpoint of this text? ◆ What is the historical context of this text?
Science	◆ Who wrote the text? What are their qualifications? How reliable is this text? ◆ What models does this author use to explain a phenomenon? ◆ How does this idea explain something in our physical world? ◆ How does this idea explain something in our biological world? ◆ How was the hypothesis proven or not proven?
Math	◆ Who wrote the text? What are their qualifications? How reliable is this text? ◆ How sound is this mathematical argument? What evidence supports this argument?
Language arts	◆ Who wrote the text? What are their qualifications? How reliable is this text? ◆ What choices did the author make that drives this text? ◆ Why this _____ (piece of author's craft)? Why here? ◆ How does this text support _____ theme?
Art/Music	◆ Who wrote the text? What are their qualifications? ◆ Do you like this piece? Why or why not? ◆ What techniques does the artist/musician use in this piece? ◆ What movement is this piece associated with? ◆ How is this piece connected to other pieces?

You will notice one question threaded throughout each discipline looking at the qualification of the author/creator of a text. In any discipline, students must get into the habit of examining the author in order to be savvy consumers of text of any kind (Beers & Probst, 2017).

This strategy is successful for two reasons:

1. It helps facilitate the wide reading needed for students to become content area experts (Hattie, Fisher, & Frey, 2016). By going beyond a single source (like the textbook), students are building their background knowledge on a topic, comparing information, and practicing their summary skills.

2. It helps frame research as a discipline-specific skill. By having students use one or more of the discipline-specific questions, we are helping to form the mindset needed for students to research well in a particular content area. Soon, they will be able to do this on their own—a great scaffold!

Updated Strategy #2: Placing the Mantle of the Expert on Students for Authentic Discussion

Part of addressing discipline-specific literacy is placing learning and discussion into authentic contexts. If we want students to feel like a practitioner of the discipline, we need to help them assume the mantle of an expert!

The original strategy of Mantle of the Expert had all students read the same text and then brainstorm a list of "experts" that might have an opinion about a central topic or question (Wilfong, 2014; Wilhelm, 2002). Different students take on the "mantle" of one of the experts and the audience (the rest of the students) pose questions to the experts. This strategy is a blast and I have used it with great success, especially with younger students. But with students in the middle grades and beyond, there is something about the pretense of the panel and the audience that loses a little of its charm. To combat this, a teacher of high school students adjusted this strategy (Rainey, Maher, Coupland, Franchi, & Moje, 2017). Here are the steps to make it work in your classroom:

1. Pick a central topic, question, or event that lends itself to controversy. A clear side on the topic, question, or event shouldn't be evident—even if there was an outcome (like a battle in a war), right or wrong is up for debate. Table 4.4 presents possible topics or events for each content area.

2. Gather several texts that lend a perspective to the central topic or event. This is a great place to consider the different levels of your students. Texts of a variety of lengths and types, including charts, graphs, and illustrations, can all lend themselves to help "answer" this question. In an ideal world, one text would be given to each student. However, in the real world, more than one student could share the same text. Table 4.2 presents a central question along with a variety of texts that could be used to help answer this question.

3. Distribute one text per student. Allow time for students to read and analyze their text and to perhaps research the author. If more than

one student shares a text, students could meet to discuss how their author feels about the central topic, question, or event.

4. Ask students to assume the mantle of the expert they have been reading about. The central topic, question, or event is posed. Students weigh in, not as themselves, but as the expert they have been studying (Rainey et al., 2017). For example, the first time students speak, they would introduce themselves as the author and perhaps give a brief introduction as to why they are an expert on this topic ("Greetings. My name is E. Percy Moran. I painted "The Battle of New Orleans").

5. After different perspectives are heard from and debated, the moderator can sum up the discussion and asks students to step out from their mantles and come to a decision based on the evidence they have heard.

After this strategy is implemented, students are primed for evidence-based writing and perhaps for even more research to back up their point of view—a win-win for all!

Table 4.4 Sample Central Topics, Questions, or Events

Content Area	Sample Central Topics, Questions, or Events
Social studies	◆ Is Andrew Jackson a hero or villain? ◆ Was the Vietnam War successful? ◆ Marco Polo changed human history.
Science	◆ Is global warming real? ◆ Most erosion is man-made. ◆ Better living is possible through chemistry.
Math	◆ What is the best way to represent data? ◆ How is thinking algebraically different from thinking arithmetically? ◆ Models are the best representation of mathematical ideas.
Language arts	◆ Mark Twain is the essential American author. ◆ Should classical literature be included in the modern English classroom? ◆ Young adult literature is the best literature for students in middle school and high school to read.
Art/Music	◆ Art can be judged as "good" and "bad." ◆ The Harlem Renaissance changed American music. ◆ Art appreciation can be taught.

Figure 4.1 Sample Central Question with Sample Texts (Social Studies Example)

Central Question: *Is Andrew Jackson a hero or villain?*
Sample texts: Painting: "The Battle of New Orleans," E. Percy Morgan 　　　　　"The Trail of Tears," Robert Lindneux Web-based articles: "10 Things You May Not Know about Andrew Jackson" 　　　　　(history.com) 　　　　　"Andrew Jackson" (biography.com) 　　　　　"Andrew Jackson, tough as old hickory" (thehermitage.com) 　　　　　"Andrew Jackson, America's original anti-establishment 　　　　　president" (smithsonianmag.com) 　　　　　"The Cherokee Trail of Tears" (legendsofAmerica.com) 　　　　　"The Cherokees vs. Andrew Jackson" (Smithsonianmag.com)

Common Core Connection

The strategies in this chapter support several of the Common Core State Standards for Literacy in History/Social Studies, Science, & Technical Subjects:

Reading Standards (History/Social Studies)

6–8	9–10	11–12
6–8.1 Cite specific textual evidence to support analysis of primary and secondary sources. 6–8.2 Determine the central ideas or information of a primary or secondary source; provide an accurate summary of the source distinct from prior knowledge or opinions.	9–10.1 Cite specific textual evidence to support analysis of primary and secondary sources, attending to such features as the date and origin of the information. 9–10.2 Determine the central ideas or information of a primary or secondary source; provide an accurate summary of how key events or ideas develop over the course of the text.	11–12.1 Cite specific textual evidence to support analysis of primary and secondary sources, connecting insights gained from specific details to an understanding of the text as a whole. 11–12.2 Determine the central ideas or information of a primary or secondary source; provide an accurate summary that makes clear the relationships among the key details and ideas.

6–8	9–10	11–12
6–8.3 Identify key steps in a text's description of a process related to history/social studies (e.g., how a bill becomes law, how interest rates are raised or lowered).	9–10.3 Analyze in detail a series of events described in a text; determine whether earlier events caused later ones or simply preceded them.	11–12.3 Evaluate various explanations for actions or events and determine which explanation best accords with textual evidence, acknowledging where the text leaves matters uncertain.
6–8.6 Identify aspects of a text that reveal an author's point of view or purpose (e.g., loaded language, inclusion or avoidance of particular facts).	9–10.6 Compare the point of view of two or more authors for how they treat the same or similar topics, including which details they include and emphasize in their respective accounts.	11–12.6 Evaluate authors' differing points of view on the same historical event or issue by assessing the authors' claims, reasoning, and evidence.
6–8.7 Integrate visual information (e.g., in charts, graphs, photographs, videos, or maps) with other information in print and digital texts.	9–10.7 Integrate quantitative or technical analysis (e.g., charts, research data) with qualitative analysis in print or digital text.	11–12.7 Integrate and evaluate multiple sources of information presented in diverse formats and media (e.g., visually, quantitatively, as well as in words) in order to address a question or solve a problem.
6–8.8 Distinguish among fact, opinion, and reasoned judgment in a text.	9–10.8 Assess the extent to which the reasoning and evidence in a text support the author's claims.	11–12.8 Evaluate an author's premises, claims, and evidence by corroborating or challenging them with other information.
6–8.9 Analyze the relationship between a primary and secondary source on the same topic.	9–10.9 Compare and contrast treatments of the same topic in several primary and secondary sources.	11–12.9 Integrate information from diverse sources, both primary and secondary, into a coherent understanding of an idea or event, noting discrepancies among sources.
6–8.10 By the end of grade 8, read and comprehend history/social studies texts in the grades 6–8 text complexity band independently and proficiently.	9–10.10 By the end of grade 10, read and comprehend history/social studies texts in the grades 9–10 text complexity band independently and proficiently.	11–12.10 By the end of grade 12, read and comprehend history/social studies texts in the grades 11-CCR text complexity band independently and proficiently.

Reading Standards (Science & Technical Subjects)

6–8	9–10	11–12
6–8.1 Cite specific textual evidence to support analysis of science and technical texts. 6–8.2 Determine the central ideas or conclusions of a text; provide an accurate summary of the text distinct from prior knowledge or opinions. 6–8.6 Analyze the author's purpose in providing an explanation, describing a procedure, or discussing an experiment in a text. 6–8.7 Integrate quantitative or technical information expressed in words in a text with a version of that information expressed visually (e.g., in a flowchart, diagram, model, graph, or table). 6–8.8 Distinguish among facts, reasoned judgment based on research findings, and speculation in a text.	9–10.1 Cite specific textual evidence to support analysis of science and technical texts, attending to the precise details of explanations or descriptions. 9–10.2 Determine the central ideas or conclusions of a text; trace the text's explanation or depiction of a complex process, phenomenon, or concept; provide an accurate summary of the text. 9–10.6 Analyze the author's purpose in providing an explanation, describing a procedure, or discussing an experiment in a text, defining the question the author seeks to address. 9–10.8 Assess the extent to which the reasoning and evidence in a text support the author's claim or a recommendation for solving a scientific or technical problem.	11–12.1 Cite specific textual evidence to support analysis of science and technical texts, attending to important distinctions the author makes and to any gaps or inconsistencies in the account. 11–12.2 Determine the central ideas or conclusions of a text; summarize complex concepts, processes, or information presented in a text by paraphrasing them in simpler but still accurate terms. context relevant to *grades 11–12 texts and topics.* 11–12.6 Analyze the author's purpose in providing an explanation, describing a procedure, or discussing an experiment in a text, identifying important issues that remain unresolved. 11–12.7 Integrate and evaluate multiple sources of information presented in diverse

6–8	9–10	11–12
6–8.9 Compare and contrast the information gained from experiments, simulations, video, or multimedia sources with that gained from reading a text on the same topic. 6–8.10 By the end of grade 8, read and comprehend science/technical texts in the grades 6–8 text complexity band independently and proficiently.	9–10.9 Compare and contrast findings presented in a text to those from other sources (including their own experiments), noting when the findings support or contradict previous explanations or accounts. 9–10.10 By the end of grade 10, read and comprehend science/technical texts in the grades 9–10 text complexity band independently and proficiently.	formats and media (e.g., quantitative data, video, multimedia) in order to address a question or solve a problem. 11–12.8 Evaluate the hypotheses, data, analysis, and conclusions in a science or technical text, verifying the data when possible and corroborating or challenging conclusions with other sources of information. 11–12.9 Synthesize information from a range of sources (e.g., texts, experiments, simulations) into a coherent understanding of a process, phenomenon, or concept, resolving conflicting information when possible. 11–12.10 By the end of grade 12, read and comprehend science/technical texts in the grades 11-CCR text complexity band independently and proficiently.

Writing Standards (History/Social Studies/Science/Other Technical Subjects)

6–8	9–10	11–12
6–8.7 Conduct short research projects to answer a question (including a self-generated question), drawing on several sources and generating additional related, focused questions that allow for multiple avenues of exploration. 6–8.8 Gather relevant information from multiple print and digital sources, using search terms effectively; assess the credibility and accuracy of each source; and quote or paraphrase the data and conclusions of others while avoiding plagiarism and following a standard format for citations. 6–8.9 Draw evidence from informational texts to support analysis, reflection, and research.	9–10.7 Conduct short as well as more sustained research projects to answer a question (including a self-generated question) or solve a problem; narrow or broaden the inquiry when appropriate; synthesize multiple sources on the subject, demonstrating understanding of the subject under investigation. 9–10.8 Gather relevant information from multiple authoritative print and digital sources, using advanced searches effectively; assess the usefulness of each source in answering the research question; integrate information into the text selectively to maintain the flow of ideas, avoiding plagiarism and following a standard format for citation. 9–10.9 Draw evidence from informational texts to support analysis, reflection, and research.	11–12.7 Conduct short as well as more sustained research projects to answer a question (including a self-generated question) or solve a problem; narrow or broaden the inquiry when appropriate; synthesize multiple sources on the subject, demonstrating understanding of the subject under investigation. 11–12.8 Gather relevant information from multiple authoritative print and digital sources, using advanced searches effectively; assess the strengths and limitations of each source in terms of the specific task, purpose, and audience; integrate information into the text selectively to maintain the flow of ideas, avoiding plagiarism and overreliance on any one source and following a standard format for citation. 11–12.9 Draw evidence from informational texts to support analysis, reflection, and research.

Action Steps

Get ready to address your students as scholars of your discipline! It is time to take some action . . .

1) Take on the challenge presented in the opening anecdote and gather the texts that students will read in your class or across a grade level team during a quarter in one place. Remember, texts can be more than the textbook or article—gather anything that students will need to interpret.

   a. Are you surprised by the amount of texts you gathered? Why or why not?

   b. Make a list of the range of texts that students will read:

      i.

      ii.

      iii.

      iv.

      v.

      vi.

      vii.

      viii.

2) Think about the type of reading that takes place in your classroom in conjunction with Table 4.1 on p. 65. What type of reading purposes do you use most in your classroom? Are there any missing from the list?

_____

_____

_____

_____

_____

_____

_____

3) Set up a sample I-Chart to use for the reading of multiple texts in your content area; include the questions you want answers to and find the resources you would use:

Student Name	Question #1	Question #2	Question #3
What I already know about this topic			
Resource #1:			
Resource #2:			
Resource #3:			
Summary across sources:			

4) What is a central topic, question, or event you could use to implement the adjusted Mantle of the Expert strategy?

_____

_____

_____

5) Find sources that students could use to assume the mantle of an expert to participate in the discussion:

i.

ii.

iii.

iv.

v.

vi.

vii.

viii.

Works Cited

Beers, K., & Probst, R. (2017). *Disrupting thinking: Why how we read matters*. New York, NY: Scholastic.

Cleaver, S. (2018, February 07). Going beyond PIE: 5 ways to teach students how to find the author's purpose. Retrieved from www.weareteachers.com/going-beyond-pie-5-ways-to-teach-students-how-to-find-the-authors-purpose/

Fisher, D., & Frey, N. (2017). Modeling disciplinary thinking. *Educational Leadership*, *74*, 82–83.

Hattie, J., Fisher, D., & Frey, N. (2016). *Visible learning for literacy, grades K-12: Implementing the practices that accelerate student learning*. New York, NY: Corwin.

Johnson, H., & Watson, P. (2011). What it is they do: Differentiating knowledge and literacy practices across content disciplines. *Journal of Adolescent and Adult Literacy*, *55*, 100–109.

Lapp, D., Grant, M., Moss, B., & Johnson, K. (2013). Students' close reading of science texts: What's now? What's next? *The Reading Teacher*, *67*, 109–119.

Moje, E. (2015). Doing and teaching disciplinary literacy with adolescent learners: A social and cultural enterprise. *Harvard Educational Review*, *85*, 254–278.

Rainey, E., Maher, B., Coupland, D., Franchi, R., & Moje, E. (2017). But what does it look like? Illustrations of disciplinary literacy teaching in two content areas. *Journal of Adolescent and Adult Literacy*, *61*, 371–379.

Siebert, D., Draper, R., Barney, D., Broomhead, P., Grierson, S., Jensen, A., Nielson, J., Nokes, J., Shumway, S., & Wimmer, J. (2016). Characteristics of literacy instruction that support reform in content area classrooms. *Journal of Adolescent and Adult Literacy*, *60*, 26–33.

Smagorinsky, P. (2001). If meaning is constructed, what is it made from? Toward a cultural theory of reading. *Review of Educational Research*, *71*, 133–169.

Wilfong, L. (2014). *Nonfiction strategies that work Do this—Not that!* New York, NY: Routledge.

Wilhelm, J. (2002). *Action strategies for deepening comprehension: Using drama strategies to assist reading performance*. New York, NY: Scholastic.

I-Chart

Student Name	Question #1	Question #2	Question #3
What I already know about this topic			
Resource #1:			
Resource #2:			
Resource #3:			
Summary across resources:			

Chapter 5

Use Content Area Vocabulary in Meaningful Ways

"I have to show you this," the teacher said, coming up to me during a break of a professional development session. He hoisted his laptop onto the table and scrolled through a document on his screen. "I was literally just listening to you say that we shouldn't assign words for students to just look up definitions of and feeling bad because that is what I left for my substitute." I nodded and smiled, appreciating the honesty. "Well, my students are turning in their definitions via Google Classroom and look what this one kid did." We both examined the screen. I realized I was reading the vocabulary words in English but seeing the definitions in Spanish. I looked up at the teacher: "Oh, is she learning English?" He shook his head 'no' emphatically: "No, she was paying so little attention to what she was doing that she copied the Spanish definitions in the back of the book instead of the English." He closed the laptop with a snap. "Obviously, this isn't a good strategy for helping them learn my vocabulary terms."

Why Is This Item on the List So Important?

Want to open up a can of worms? Bring up the concept of vocabulary instruction with a group of teachers and watch the sparks fly. If there are 30 teachers in the room, then there will be 30 different opinions on how to best instruct vocabulary. While some will still be using the "assign and define" method, as illustrated (and hopefully debunked!) in the anecdote above, others will argue for a variety of worksheets, graphic organizers, and more to teach important words.

While we don't have to agree about how we teach vocabulary, we do have to agree that vocabulary is primary to our goals as teachers of readers and writers. It is a predictor of reading comprehension and reading comprehension test scores (Baumann, Kame'enui, & Ash, 2003; Berninger, Abbott, Nagy, & Carlisle, 2010; Reutzel & Cooter, 2015). And while its importance is undeniable, far too many teachers continue to use old-fashioned vocabulary strategies that students see as meaningless and boring (Rasinski, Padak, & Newton, 2017; Wilfong, 2012).

I have written an entire book dedicated to the do this—not that principle of vocabulary instruction (Wilfong, 2012). The ideas I wrote about then are true now; here are a few of my favorites:

1. Select and instruct words with purpose.
2. Go beyond memorization by having students apply meanings in context.
3. Assess the use of vocabulary words through authentic speaking and writing.
4. Allow students to use images in conjunction with learning new vocabulary words.
5. Create and use a word wall with purpose in every classroom.

This chapter in this book will focus particularly on making vocabulary instruction work in the abbreviated time frame so many content area teachers have.

> **"Do this, not that" principle #5**: *DO use content area vocabulary in meaningful ways. DON'T assign vocabulary to study without attending to why and how words are selected and practiced.*

To Get Started

The selection of vocabulary words for instruction is a process easy to pass off onto textbook publishers/curriculum creators. But one of the first ways we can take control of vocabulary instruction in our classrooms is to take a hard look at what words we are spending our time on. When I initially researched how textbook publishers select the words listed at the beginning of a chapter,

I was astounded to find out that most publishers (who freely offered up this information!) chose words that appeared more than once and were multi-syllabic (Wilfong, 2012). I don't know about you, but long words that appear a bunch of times is not the scientific answer I was hoping for! Luckily for us, there are two more scientific ways to help teachers take a hard look at those lists and select the ones that really make sense for our students.

When I run workshops on vocabulary, I ask teachers to either bring or brainstorm a list of vocabulary words that they might teach in conjunction with a particular unit or text. They can then run these two words through one of the following processes:

1. *Tiering words to find the focus*. First introduced by Beck, McKeown, and Kucan (2013), this simple strategy allows teachers to separate a list of words into three tiers to help decide where the instructional focus should be. Table 5.1 explains the difference between the three tiers.

Words that fall into Tier 1, everyday words, are words that most students should know and do not require direct instruction on. However, in this category, I am always aware of my English Language Learners. Words that I might think are Tier 1 might be new to a student new to the English language. Frontload these words with pictures for these students!

Tier 2 words, polysemic or multiple-meaning words, give students power over words whose meaning changes depending on the context. These words are powerful for instructional focus. Tier 2 words are the terms that I recommend for direct instruction and use with strategies to help students expand their vocabularies. Time spent in the classroom on vocabulary strategies can be used in conjunction with these words.

Now, as a content area teacher, you might be more inclined to focus on Tier 3 words, or words that are discipline-specific, for vocabulary instruction. However, these are the terms that are important for student comprehension right off the bat. Rather than using instructional time for working on the meaning of these words, give students access to these definitions and a picture or symbol to accompany the word. Go over them briefly and then move on with life. Immediate access to these words becomes immediate access to your content.

Table 5.1 The Three Tiers of Vocabulary Instruction

Tier	Definition
Tier 1	Everyday words, easily picked up from interactions with others
Tier 2	Multiple-meaning words; meaning changes depending on the context
Tier 3	Discipline-specific words; only one meaning

Last word on the tiers: If you don't have a lot of words in the Tier 2 category, take a close look at your Tier 3 words. Do any of them have a Greek or Latin root hidden within? If so, move it to Tier 2. In updated strategy #1, below, you will see how these Greek or Latin roots can help generate more words!

2. *Applying the Frey and Fisher (2009) questions to find words for instruction.* If tiering seems too simple, or you have tried tiering before and are ready for something else, I find that running a set of words through Frey and Fisher's (2009) questions to determine which words to teach is a more in-depth process to use. These twelve questions, divided into six categories, really help teachers answer the question: Why I am teaching this word? Table 5.2 presents the six categories along with their associated questions.

With these questions handy, I recommend setting up a table like that in Table 5.3 to analyze your list and whittle it down to those that truly deserve instruction. Teachers can place check marks across the table if the answer to

Table 5.2 Frey and Fisher's Questions for Vocabulary Selection

Category	Question(s)
Representative	◆ Is the word representative of a family of words that students should know? ◆ Is the concept represented by the word critical to understanding the text? ◆ Is the word a label for an idea that students need to know? ◆ Does the word represent an idea that is essential for understanding another concept?
Repeatability	◆ Will the word be used again in this text? If so, does the word occur often enough to be redundant? ◆ Will the word be used again during the school year?
Transportable	◆ Will the word be used in group discussions? ◆ Will the word be used in writing tasks? ◆ Will the word be used in other content or subject areas?
Contextual Analysis	◆ Can students use context clues to determine the correct or intended meaning of the word without instruction?
Structural Analysis	◆ Can students use structural analysis to determine the correct or intended meaning of the word without instruction?
Cognitive Load	◆ Have I identified too many words for students to successfully integrate?

Table 5.3 Sample Analysis Table for Frey and Fisher's Questions

Vocabulary List	Representative	Repeatabillity	Transportable	Contextual Analysis	Structural Analysis
Word 1					
Word 2					
Word 3					
Word 4					
Word 5					
Word 6					

the question or the majority of the questions in each category is "yes." For the first three categories, a check mark means that this word needs direct instruction. For the final three categories, a check mark means that this word can be figured out by most students through the use of context clues, Greek or Latin roots, or that too many words (8–12 per week!) has been reached.

Whichever process you prefer, my plea to you is to use *some* process to select your words for instruction. Whether you focus on Tier 2 words or the words pointed out through the Frey and Fisher questions, then you have done your due diligence in making sure you are teaching words that are necessary! Some of the best teacher-based team meetings I have been a part of have been applying one of these processes to a list of words for an upcoming unit. The conversations that ensue are truly intelligent discourse by teachers about what to teach!

Instructional Practices to Update

Updated Strategy #1: Using a Generative Approach to Building Vocabularies

Starting in first grade, the study of Greek and Latin roots to help define unknown words appears in the standards (CCSS, 2010). And for good reason! A single root can give access to an average of 20 other words (Rasinski et al., 2017; Wilfong, 2012). In fact, as many as 70% of words in the English language have a Greek or Latin root (Nagy & Anderson, 1984). As a word attack skill, Greek and Latin roots allow students to tackle parts of words to divine meaning. Rather than giving the arbitrary directive, "Use your context clues to figure out any words you don't know!" Greek or Latin roots help students dig into words for parts they know: "Do you see an affix within that word that you know? How can that help you figure out a new word?"

A generative approach to teaching vocabulary relies upon those words that you moved from Tier 3 to Tier 2 that have a Greek or Latin root within. These discipline-specific words are the key to helping students build their vocabularies, both in your content and beyond, discussing the affix within the word, and then *generating* other words that have this root.

Flanigan, Templeton, and Hayes (2012) like the use of a root web to help students generate words. In this strategy, a Tier 3 word with a Greek or Latin root is identified and placed in the outer circle. The root itself is placed in the center (and defined). Students then brainstorm other words that have this root. Words outside the content area are allowed! The idea is that this helps students see the connection between this language skill and content area words they find.

The original word in Figure 5.1 was "dissect," taken from a fifth-grade science unit about to embark on a lab that required students to dissect a worm. The teacher presented what the root "sect" meant, placed "dissect" in the web, and the students went nuts coming up with new words that contained the root and puzzling through their meanings with this new knowledge. As one student yelled out, "It's like being given a cheat sheet to help you figure out words!" The teacher and I grinned at each other from across the room.

To take this strategy a step further, students could be pressed to try to brainstorm words that contain the root across the content areas (Flanigan, Templeton, & Hayes, 2012). Figure 5.2 presents this template, a great challenge for students learning to apply root word knowledge. Blank templates for both strategies are included at the end of the chapter.

Figure 5.1 Sample Root Web

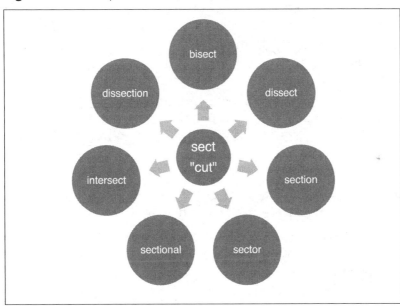

Figure 5.2 Root Words across the Content Areas

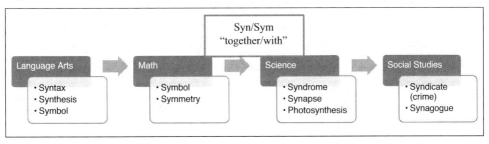

Updated Strategy #2: Moving from Memorization to Application When Learning New Words

A big gigantic "do this, not that": If you are still having students take any kind of matching test to prove that they know the meaning of words, stop! Beyond your local Bureau of Motor Vehicles, matching tests are an obsolete way of showing learning. As one eighth grader recently confided to me after a matching test of social studies terms, "If I know a few of them, I can generally guess the rest." He grinned up at me. "I'm good at guessing games."

The truest application of learning a new word is the ability to *use* it. The first step in becoming an "owner" of a new word is the ability to use it when speaking. This oral rehearsal allows us to safely try out a new word as we grapple with its part of speech, its meaning, and how to weave it into sentences. The ultimate sophistication in learning a new word is the ability to write with it. To take a new word and work it into an essay or response (and use it correctly!) is higher-order thinking at work. Writing with new vocabulary helps a learner move from generalizations about content ("The cloud was white and fluffy") to sounding like an expert about content ("The cloud can be classified as cumulus").

Radio News—providing opportunities for oral rehearsal and writing of new terms
On my drive into work today, I listened to terrestrial radio for the local news. News on the radio is different from the morning or evening news on television; the newscaster has to be concise to cram a lot information into a two-minute blip. Yet, in that quick blip, they sound like an expert. This format is perfect for allowing students to try out new terms, while also practicing their summarizing and writing terms. Here's how to make it happen:

1. Gather texts/bookmark resources for use around a topic relevant to a unit currently under study. Even the textbook can serve as a resource for the Radio News!

2. Play a few clips of the news from a local radio station for students. Point out the vocabulary used and the brevity of the clip.

3. Model turning a content area topic into a radio clip. Figure 5.3 shows a model from a sixth-grade social studies class, using the Radio News template (a blank template is provided at the end of the chapter).

4. Assign topics or allow students to choose a topic within the unit. Ask students to identify terms that they need to include in their news clip to sounds like "experts" of the topic.

5. Have students prepare a script of their "news." Summarizing skills are in full effect!

Figure 5.3   Radio News Sample

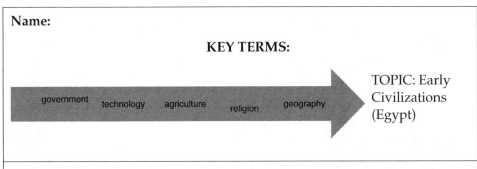

Name:

KEY TERMS:

government   technology   agriculture   religion   geography

TOPIC: Early
Civilizations
(Egypt)

Script:

Breaking news! Archeologists have learned a ton about why early
civilizations like that of the Egyptians flourished. The geography of the
civilization was important because it was near the Nile River. This also
helped agriculture because there was very fertile soil. And can you believe
it? Technologies like irrigation and roads helped spread the Egyptian
civilization. Their government was established to help address the needs
of the culture. An interesting tidbit is that the Egyptians worshipped many
gods. Thanks and have a great day!

6. Record student scripts! GarageBand (Macs), Audacity, and even just
   the Voice Recorder on a typical phone can all be used for recording.

7. Gather all the "news" in one place. Students can now use these to
   review key concepts and terms.

Fluency, prosody, summarizing, writing informational text, AND
vocabulary—this simple strategy hits several standards.

Updated Strategy #3: Using Technology to Bring Vocabulary to Life

Two new technologies bring fun to the practice of vocabulary terms beyond
basic worksheets:

1. Flipgrid (www.flipgrid.com) is a free, shared space for students
   to record and upload 90-second videos. After the teacher creates
   an account, they set up a prompt and a password for students to
   access their space. In a recent professional development session
   with teachers of English Language Learners, I chose a science unit of
   study focusing on earthquakes. Terms like plate tectonics, epicenter,
   magnitude, Richter scale, and more were passed out to teachers on

notecards. In small groups of three to four, they had to come up with a 90-second (or less!) video explaining their word to others. The only rule was this—they couldn't just record themselves reciting the definition. Teachers wrote and read Readers' Theatres, acted out the word, and created and explained models to teach about their word. After 15 minutes, all the videos were recorded in either the Flipgrid app or through the website. Highlights of Flipgrid include a place for a rubric to grade the videos, optional commenting for students, similar to Instagram or Facebook, and, most importantly, all vocabulary terms are gathered and explained in one spot for students to use for review.

2. Padlet (www.padlet.com), like Flipgrid, is a gathering space for information but instead of videos, the information comes in the form of electronic sticky notes. The teacher creates a (free) account and then poses a central prompt or question that students can access via an emailed link or QR code. While this is such a great way to do entrance and exit slips (more on those in Chapter 7), they also work to crowd-source vocabulary terms. Assign each student a term and give them access to the Padlet. Like a GoogleDoc, students can work on the site at the same time. Students create their "sticky," explaining their term in prose, picture, or a link—or all three! At the end of a few short minutes, all students have the definitions of important terms in one place. Brilliant!

Common Core Connection

The strategies in this chapter specifically support the vocabulary standards in reading (standard four) and writing (standard D in informative writing) across History/Social Studies, Science, & Technical Subjects.

Reading Standards (History/Social Studies)

6–8	9–10	11–12
6–8.4 Determine the meaning of words and phrases as they are used in a text, including vocabulary specific to domains related to history/social studies.	9–10.4 Determine the meaning of words and phrases as they are used in a text, including vocabulary describing political, social, or economic aspects of history/social science.	11–12.4 Determine the meaning of words and phrases as they are used in a text, including analyzing how an author uses and refines the meaning of a key term over the course of a text (e.g., how Madison defines *faction* in *Federalist* No. 10).

Reading Standards (Science & Technical Subjects)

6–8	9–10	11–12
6–8.4 Determine the meaning of symbols, key terms, and other domain-specific words and phrases as they are used in a specific scientific or technical context relevant to *grades 6–8 texts and topics*.	9–10.4 Determine the meaning of symbols, key terms, and other domain-specific words and phrases as they are used in a specific scientific or technical context relevant to *grades 9–10 texts and topics*.	11–12.4 Determine the meaning of symbols, key terms, and other domain-specific words and phrases as they are used in a specific scientific or technical context relevant to *grades 11–12 texts and topics*.

Writing Standards (History/Social Studies/Science/Other Technical Subjects)

6–8	9–10	11–12
6–8.2D Use precise language and domain-specific vocabulary to inform about or explain the topic.	9–10.2D Use precise language and domain-specific vocabulary to manage the complexity of the topic and convey a style appropriate to the discipline and context as well as to the expertise of likely readers.	11–12.2D Use precise language, domain-specific vocabulary and techniques such as metaphor, simile, and analogy to manage the complexity of the topic; convey a knowledgeable stance in a style that responds to the discipline and context as well as to the expertise of likely readers.

Action Steps

Grab a list of vocabulary terms that you usually teach in conjunction with an upcoming unit—it's time to take some action . . .

1) Try out both tiering and using the Fisher and Frey questions on your vocabulary list.

a. Which process did you like better? Why? _____

_____

_____

b. Which process gave you better information about which words to focus on? Why? _____

_____

_____

2) Choose one of your vocabulary terms that has a Greek or Latin root:

_____

a. First, identify and define your root: _____

_____

b. Now, create a Root Web for your word. How many other words were you able to generate from your root? _____

c. Bonus! Take your root across the curriculum—how many other content area words are you able to find using that same root?

_____

3) Brainstorm a list of topics that students could create Radio News broadcasts around for an upcoming unit:

a.

b.

c.

d.

e.

f.

g.

4) Which technology could you see yourself using in conjunction with teaching vocabulary, Flipgrid or Padlet? Why?

_____

_____

_____

Works Cited

Baumann, J., Kame'enui, E., & Ash, G. (2003). Research on vocabulary instruction: Voltaire redux. In J. Flood, D. Lapp, J. R. Squire, & J. M. Jensen (Eds.), *Handbook of research on teaching the English Language Arts* (2nd ed., pp. 752–785). Mahwah, NJ: Erlbaum.

Beck, I., McKeown, M., & Kucan, L. (2013). *Bringing words to life: Robust vocabulary instruction* (2nd ed.). New York, NY: Guilford Press.

Berninger, V., Abbott, R., Nagy, W., & Carlisle, J. (2010). Growth in phonological, orthographic, and morphological awareness in grades 1 to 6. *Journal of Psycholinguistic Research*, *39*, 141–163.

Nagy, W. E., & Anderson, R. C. (1984). How many words are there in printed school English? *Reading Research Quarterly*, *19*(3), 304–330.

National Governors Association Center for Best Practices & Council of Chief State School Officers. (2010). *Common Core State Standards for English Language Arts*. Washington, DC: Authors.

Flanigan, K., Templeton, S., & Hayes, L. (2012). What's in a word? Using content vocabulary to *generate* growth in general academic vocabulary knowledge. *Journal of Adolescent and Adult Literacy*, *56*, 132–140.

Frey, N., & Fisher, D. (2009). *Learning words inside and out: Vocabulary instruction that boosts achievement in all subject areas*. Portsmouth, NH: Heinemann.

Rasinski, T., Padak, N., & Newton, J. (2017). The roots of comprehension: Studying Greek and Latin word origins makes vocabulary instruction resonate. *Educational Leadership*, *74*(5), 41–45.

Reutzel, D., & Cooter, R. (2015). *Teaching children to read: The teacher makes the difference* (7th ed.). New York, NY: Pearson.

Wilfong, L. (2012). *Vocabulary strategies that work: Do this—not that!* New York, NY: Routledge.

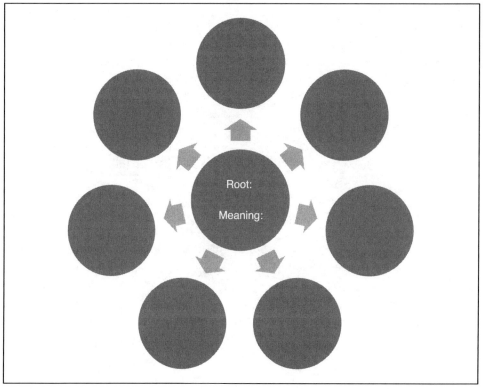

Root Words across the Content Areas

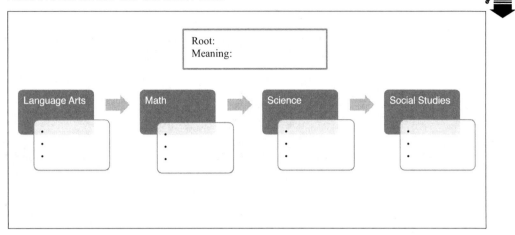

Radio News Template

Name:

KEY TERMS

TOPIC:

Script:

_____

_____

_____

_____

_____

_____

_____

_____

_____

_____

_____

_____

_____

_____

Chapter 6

Make Writing an Authentic Process in Every Classroom

For more than a year, the social studies department at a local middle school had worked to embed writing in every class. After an initial meeting with me to develop a framework that laid out expectations for daily, weekly, and unit writing, I had the opportunity to visit classrooms towards the end of the year. At the beginning of one class, the students sat down and immediately took out their notebooks to respond to a prompt on the board. "Entrance slip time!" the teacher sang out. One student responded, "We write more in here than we do in English!" The teacher shot back, looking at me across the room, "Mission accomplished."

Why Is This Item on the List So Important?

In a brief, not-at-all scientific survey of content area teachers (i.e. an email I sent to friends of mine that teach either science or social studies at the middle or high school level), I discovered that out of ten teachers, only one of them had any writing instruction as part of their teacher preparation program. As one individual put it to me: "I think it was one hour of one class meeting of a three-hour-per week, 16-week class. Is that enough?"

With numbers like these, it is no wonder that many teachers shy away from writing. And if they do include writing, it is more likely to be short, one-to-two sentence responses (Education Trust, 2015).

Table 6.1   A Framework for Writing across the Content Areas

Daily	Weekly	Unit/Quarterly
◆ Entrance Slips ◆ Exit Slips ◆ Written Conversations ◆ Quick Writes/Prompts ◆ Learning Logs	◆ Summaries ◆ Extended Response ◆ CREW-C Arguments ◆ Found Poetry	◆ Essays ◆ Reports ◆ Multigenre Projects

When the Common Core State Standards came out in 2010, they made the bold move of including literacy standards for history/social studies, science, and technical subjects (CCSS, 2010). Teachers from all disciplines nodded their heads in agreement with the reading standards. This was the kind of work that they had been implementing in their classrooms for years—summaries, vocabulary study, comprehension strategies (Fisher, Brozo, Frey, & Ivey, 2014; Vacca, Vacca, & Mraz, 2013). It was the writing standards that grabbed attention; teachers from all disciplines were being asked to write argumentative and informative pieces in grades 6–12 (CCSS, 2010; see standards listed at the end of this chapter). *These* made teachers sit up straight.

Writing in all content areas has to be more than essays and reports. It needs to include daily, short strategies that get students thinking about content through writing (addressed in Chapter 7); weekly, slightly longer pieces that synthesize learning (addressed in Chapter 8); and yes, those essays and reports that capture the heart of informative and argumentative writing standards (addressed in Chapters 9 and 10). Table 6.1 lays out a framework for writing in all disciplines, divided by daily, weekly, and unit/quarterly writing assignments.

"Do this, not that" principle #6: DO make writing an authentic process in every classroom. DON'T force writing in your classroom.

To Get Started

Why writing? Writing is thinking (Bambrick-Santoyo & Chiger, 2017; Gallagher, 2017). When you put pen or pencil to paper, you are making the ideas that are floating around in your brain come to concrete life. But more than that, writing helps to generate new ideas (Langer & Applebee, 1987). The moment you write something down and then read it to yourself, you are almost always intrinsically prompted to add to it—you can't help it! I tried this recently with a group of preservice teachers:

> *Me:* On a blank piece of paper, at the top, write down the name of your favorite athlete.
> [students writing]
> *Me:* Okay, share what you wrote with the person sitting next to you.

I teach in Northeast Ohio, home to the Cleveland Cavaliers, so almost everyone wrote down LeBron James. But here is where the generating of new ideas took place, without prompting: all but two of the seventeen students I had in class had started to add words they use to describe Lebron—superstar, MVP, better than Curry—just by beginning the process with my simple prompt, I was able to show how writing is a generative act.

Teachers may argue that good oral discussion is deep thinking but it never reaches the depth that writing does (Bambrick-Santoyo & Chiger, 2017). There are a few reasons why writing tops discussion for thinking:

♦ *Writing means that 100% of students can participate.* So often during class discussions, a few students dominate the discourse. This allows students who are not prepared or who simply do not want to participate an "out" that allows them to sit passively.

♦ *Writing honors different speeds of thinking.* By giving students time to process information and then write, we allow slower, more reflective thinkers time to catch up with their speedier counterparts. Students sometimes report not participating in class discussions because they were working on their wording or ideas in their heads but class discussion moved too fast.

♦ *Writing provides teachers with evidence of student learning.* This may be personal, but I was never great at keeping anecdotal notes to document student learning during discussion. Having students write something, even a few sentences, allowed me to assess student learning and plan my next instructional move.

Planning for instruction. As you work to make writing a part of your classroom, consider the following:

♦ *Choice matters.* As students are working to understand how writing works in all disciplines, some modicum of choice can help them feel ownership of the writing process. Too often, writing is something that is "done" to students in content area classes (write this lab, analyze this primary source). Allowing students to explore what they want to write about (within a topic or unit) can help open up students to the kind of writing that is important in each content area.

- *Audience matters.* In discipline-specific writing, audience is central. Helping students define a clear audience for their writing (Other scientists? Historians? Mathematicians? Politicians?), whether by assignment or choice, helps students clarify their purpose for writing.

- *Meaning matters.* Are you having students just answer questions to show they understand a reading? Or are they writing to construct real meaning?—to think, reflect, analyze, and synthesize information (Vermont Writing Collaborative, 2016).

- *Organization matters.* Most content area writing has a specific structure or framework to organize ideas that students do not learn through osmosis. Direct instruction of these structures assists students in finding a "vehicle for thinking" (Vermont Writing Collaborative, 2016).

- *Frequency matters.* There is a direct correlation between the amount of writing students do and how well students write (National Writing Project & Nagin, 2006).

Instructional Practices to Update

Updated Strategy #1: Set Ground Rules for Writing in Your Classroom

One of the first questions I get from content area teachers about writing is about the requirements: What exactly should I require from students when I have them write in my classroom? This is an important conversation that needs to happen in departments, across instructional teams, over the whole school! If Student A is required to write complete sentences and with correct conventions in one class but is allowed to write phrases and not worry about capitals and periods in another, confusion reigns! Students need to be required to write correctly and conventionally in all classes, with very few exceptions. A few ground rules:

1. *Complete sentences are always required.* Unless students are creating a bulleted list of some sort or brainstorming, complete sentences (a complete thought in every sentence!) is necessary.

2. *Conventional spelling (grade-level appropriate) is always required.* This means that any word that is appropriate for the student to spell at their grade level should be spelled correctly. Words above the students' pay grade can be spelled phonetically. Text language is not appropriate unless for a specific assignment (I have one of these in Chapter 7!).

Figure 6.1 Ground Rules for Writing in Any Classroom

> 1. *Complete sentences are always required.*
> 2. *Conventional spelling (grade level appropriate) is always required.*
> 3. *Capitalize the first word of each sentence and proper nouns.*
> 4. *Include appropriate ending punctuation.*
> 5. *Write until you are done – not until you have written a certain number of sentences that your teacher tells you to write.*

3. *Capitalize the first word of each sentence and proper nouns.* Yes, all students need reminded of this every time they write. There is actual brain research showing that students *know* they need to do these things but as their brain reaches for more sophisticated writing traits, it can forget some of the basics.

4. *Include appropriate ending punctuation.* Just like number 3, students need to be reminded that sentences end with punctuation.

5. *Write until you are done—not until you have written a certain number of sentences that your teacher tells you to write.* We have to build efficacy in students when writing to end when they feel they are done . . . not after they have written the obligatory two or three (or whatever) number of sentences their teacher tells them to write. I rant (ahem), *write* about this more in Chapter 9 when talking about the writing process.

Figure 6.1 illustrates the basic rules for engagement in writing in any classroom.

Updated Strategy #2: Use Graphic Organizers AFTER Drafting

Think about your own writing processes. Prior to an email or text, or an essay for a class, do you fill out a graphic organizer? Technology is changing the way we draft. Most of us just sit at our computers and . . . go. And yet, teachers still persist in forcing every student to use a graphic organizer prior to drafting.

Let's think about the graphic organizer for a moment, shall we? When first created, the graphic organizer was intended to differentiate content. It was a way to break down content into meaningful chunks for students who had trouble arranging it for themselves (Ausubel, 1969). But somewhere along the way, graphic organizers became a blanket for all students, distributed freely by teachers. Then it became part of a checklist—I am being observed— I need to make sure I differentiate! So, a graphic organizer is employed. And yet, the way it is used is not differentiating at all . . . it is compliance.

From its original intention to differentiate, graphic organizers became a writing checkpoint. Teachers used the t-chart, the web, the spoke and wheel as a way to check if students were ready to draft. A completed graphic organizer signaled that the student was ready to proceed with actual writing.

Want to make me really mad? Then have students use a graphic organizer to fill out a graphic organizer. I have been in classrooms where students have to fill out a web and then turn that web into an outline for the paper. By the time the student goes to write the paper, they have already written their evidence TWICE. No wonder so many of our students dislike writing!

We need to get back to the original purpose of the graphic organizer—using it as a tool for differentiation in writing. I am happy to support teaching students about various graphic organizers that help organize thoughts while writing but I urge teachers to do this at the beginning of the year, or unit, or teaching of a specific genre. Then, remove the scaffold and allow students to choose whether they wish to complete a graphic organizer prior to writing. It allows the student to think about their writing needs.

Amy Hirzel, an 11th-grade teacher in Cleveland, starts her year by having students think about their writing processes. She pushes them to go deep—technology or paper? Fonts? Pen color? Snack breaks? By the end of her class she hopes that they develop their writing process as a *writer*, not just a student trying to earn an "A."

Here is a short list of processes that writers use prior to drafting:

- Freewriting
- Listing
- Outlining (it's how I wrote this book!)
- Bullet points
- Headings
- And yes, graphic organizers

If you are so stuck on the graphic organizer idea, then flip the script. Have students draft *first*, then give them a graphic organizer to distill their work into. By writing first and then completing the graphic organizer, students are able to see where holes exist in their writing. They are also able to see where they might lack in structure or evidence. Re-writes and additions become obvious in this process.

Updated Strategy #3: Think About What It Means to Be a Writer in Your Discipline

Just like with reading, it is helpful to think about the kinds of writing that your discipline requires. Table 6.2 presents a list of structures and formats across content areas.

This list is by no means complete but a jumping-off point for thinking about the different kinds of writing you could include in your classroom as you plan.

Table 6.2 Writing Structures and Formats across the Content Areas

Social Studies	Science	Math	Art/Music	P.E./Health
– Editorials – Comparisons – Speeches – Chronology – Research report – Interviews – Cause & effect – Problem/solution	– Laboratory reports – Observations – Editorials – Commentaries – Research reports – Journal article – Scientific poster – Interviews – Research memo – Cause & effect – Problem/solution	– Explaining thinking behind a problem – Math journal – Interview – Research report – Journal article – Comparisons – Chronology	– Critique – Interview – Journal article – Research report – Comparisons – Chronology	– Description – Journal article – Research report – Interview – Comparisons

Common Core Connection

The strategies presented in this chapter address several of the Common Core Standards for writing:

Writing Standards (History/Social Studies/Science/Other Technical Subjects)

6–8	9–10	11–12

6–8.1 Write arguments focused on *discipline-specific content*.
 	
  6–8.1a Introduce claim(s) about a topic or issue, acknowledge and distinguish the claim(s) from alternate or opposing claims, and organize the reasons and evidence logically.
 	
  6–8.1b Support claim(s) with logical reasoning and relevant, accurate data and evidence that demonstrate an understanding of the topic or text, using credible sources.
 	
  6–8.1c Use words, phrases, and clauses to create cohesion and clarify the relationships among claim(s), counterclaims, reasons, and evidence.
 	
  6–8.1d Establish and maintain a formal style.
 	
  6–8.1e Provide a concluding statement or section that follows from and supports the argument presented.
	9–10.1 Write arguments focused on *discipline-specific content*.
	
	  9–10.1a Introduce precise claim(s), distinguish the claim(s) from alternate or opposing claims, and create an organization that establishes clear relationships among the claim(s), counterclaims, reasons, and evidence.
	
	  9–10.1b Develop claim(s) and counterclaims fairly, supplying data and evidence for each while pointing out the strengths and limitations of both claim(s) and counterclaims in a discipline-appropriate form and in a manner that anticipates the audience's knowledge level and concerns.
	
	  9–10.1c Use words, phrases, and clauses to link the major sections of the text, create cohesion, and clarify the relationships between claim(s) and reasons, between reasons and
		11–12.1 Write arguments focused on *discipline-specific content*.
		
		  11–12.1a Introduce precise, knowledgeable claim(s), establish the significance of the claim(s), distinguish the claim(s) from alternate or opposing claims, and create an organization that logically sequences the claim(s), counterclaims, reasons, and evidence.
		
		  11–12.1b Develop claim(s) and counterclaims fairly and thoroughly, supplying the most relevant data and evidence for each while pointing out the strengths and limitations of both claim(s) and counterclaims in a discipline-appropriate form that anticipates the audience's knowledge level, concerns, values, and possible biases.
		
		  11–12.1c Use words, phrases, and clauses as well as varied syntax to link the major sections of the text, create

6–8	9–10	11–12
6–8.2 Write informative/explanatory texts, including the narration of historical events, scientific procedures/ experiments, or technical processes. 6–8.2a Introduce a topic clearly, previewing what is to follow; organize ideas, concepts, and information into broader categories as appropriate to achieving purpose; include formatting (e.g., headings), graphics (e.g., charts, tables), and multimedia when useful to aiding comprehension. 6–8.2b Develop the topic with relevant, well-chosen facts, definitions, concrete details, quotations, or other information and examples. 6–8.2c Use appropriate and varied transitions to create cohesion and clarify the relationships among ideas and concepts. 6–8.2d Use precise language and domain-specific vocabulary to inform about or explain the topic. 6–8.2e Establish and maintain a formal style and objective tone.	evidence, and between claim(s) and counterclaims. 9–10.1d Establish and maintain a formal style and objective tone while attending to the norms and conventions of the discipline in which they are writing. 9–10.1e Provide a concluding statement or section that follows from or supports the argument presented. 9–10.2 Write informative/ explanatory texts, including the narration of historical events, scientific procedures/ experiments, or technical processes. 9–10.2a Introduce a topic and organize ideas, concepts, and information to make important connections and distinctions; include formatting (e.g., headings), graphics (e.g., figures, tables), and multimedia when useful to aiding comprehension. 9–10.2b Develop the topic with well-chosen, relevant, and sufficient facts, extended definitions, concrete details, quotations, or other information and	cohesion, and clarify the relationships between claim(s) and reasons, between reasons and evidence, and between claim(s) and counterclaims. 11–12.1d Establish and maintain a formal style and objective tone while attending to the norms and conventions of the discipline in which they are writing. 11–12.1e Provide a concluding statement or section that follows from or supports the argument presented. 11–12.2 Write informative/ explanatory texts, including the narration of historical events, scientific procedures/ experiments, or technical processes. 11–12.2a Introduce a topic and organize complex ideas, concepts, and information so that each new element builds on that which precedes it to create a unified whole; include formatting (e.g., headings), graphics (e.g., figures, tables), and multimedia when useful to aiding comprehension.

(*Continued*)

(Continued)

6–8	9–10	11–12
6–8.2f Provide a concluding statement or section that follows from and supports the information or explanation presented. 6–8.4 Produce clear and coherent writing in which the development, organization, and style are appropriate to task, purpose, and audience. 6–8.5 With some guidance and support from peers and adults, develop and strengthen writing as needed by planning, revising, editing, rewriting, or trying a new approach, focusing on how well purpose and audience have been addressed. 6–8.6 Use technology, including the Internet, to produce and publish writing and present the relationships between information and ideas clearly and efficiently. 6–8.7 Conduct short research projects to answer a question (including a self-generated question), drawing on several sources and generating additional related, focused questions that allow for multiple avenues of exploration.	examples appropriate to the audience's knowledge of the topic. 9–10.2c Use varied transitions and sentence structures to link the major sections of the text, create cohesion, and clarify the relationships among ideas and concepts. 9–10.2d Use precise language and domain-specific vocabulary to manage the complexity of the topic and convey a style appropriate to the discipline and context as well as to the expertise of likely readers. 9–10.2e Establish and maintain a formal style and objective tone while attending to the norms and conventions of the discipline in which they are writing. 9–10.2f Provide a concluding statement or section that follows from and supports the information or explanation presented (e.g., articulating implications or the significance of the topic). 9–10.4 Produce clear and coherent writing in which the development, organization, and style are appropriate to task, purpose, and audience.	11–12.2b Develop the topic thoroughly by selecting the most significant and relevant facts, extended definitions, concrete details, quotations, or other information and examples appropriate to the audience's knowledge of the topic. 11–12.2c Use varied transitions and sentence structures to link the major sections of the text, create cohesion, and clarify the relationships among complex ideas and concepts. 11–12.2d Use precise language, domain-specific vocabulary and techniques such as metaphor, simile, and analogy to manage the complexity of the topic; convey a knowledgeable stance in a style that responds to the discipline and context as well as to the expertise of likely readers. 11–12.2e Provide a concluding statement or section that follows from and supports the information or explanation provided (e.g., articulating implications or the significance of the topic).

6–8	9–10	11–12
6–8.8 Gather relevant information from multiple print and digital sources, using search terms effectively; assess the credibility and accuracy of each source; and quote or paraphrase the data and conclusions of others while avoiding plagiarism and following a standard format for citations. 6–8.9 Draw evidence from informational texts to support analysis, reflection, and research. 6–8.10 Write routinely over extended time frames (time for reflection and revision) and shorter time frames (a single sitting or a day or two) for a range of discipline-specific tasks, purposes, and audiences.	9–10.5 Develop and strengthen writing as needed by planning, revising, editing, rewriting, or trying a new approach, focusing on addressing what is most significant for a specific purpose and audience. 9–10.6 Use technology, including the Internet, to produce, publish, and update individual or shared writing products, taking advantage of technology's capacity to link to other information and to display information flexibly and dynamically. 9–10.7 Conduct short as well as more sustained research projects to answer a question (including a self-generated question) or solve a problem; narrow or broaden the inquiry when appropriate; synthesize multiple sources on the subject, demonstrating understanding of the subject under investigation.	11–12.4 Produce clear and coherent writing in which the development, organization, and style are appropriate to task, purpose, and audience. 11–12.5 Develop and strengthen writing as needed by planning, revising, editing, rewriting, or trying a new approach, focusing on addressing what is most significant for a specific purpose and audience. 11–12.6 Use technology, including the Internet, to produce, publish, and update individual or shared writing products in response to ongoing feedback, including new arguments or information. 11–12.7 Conduct short as well as more sustained research projects to answer a question (including a self-generated question) or solve a problem; narrow or broaden the inquiry when appropriate; synthesize multiple sources on the subject, demonstrating understanding of the subject under investigation.

(Continued)

6–8	9–10	11–12
	9–10.8 Gather relevant information from multiple authoritative print and digital sources, using advanced searches effectively; assess the usefulness of each source in answering the research question; integrate information into the text selectively to maintain the flow of ideas, avoiding plagiarism and following a standard format for citation. 9–10.9 Draw evidence from informational texts to support analysis, reflection, and research. 9–10.10 Write routinely over extended time frames (time for reflection and revision) and shorter time frames (a single sitting or a day or two) for a range of discipline-specific tasks, purposes, and audiences.	11–12.8 Gather relevant information from multiple authoritative print and digital sources, using advanced searches effectively; assess the strengths and limitations of each source in terms of the specific task, purpose, and audience; integrate information into the text selectively to maintain the flow of ideas, avoiding plagiarism and overreliance on any one source and following a standard format for citation. 11–12.9 Draw evidence from informational texts to support analysis, reflection, and research. 11–12.10 Write routinely over extended time frames (time for reflection and revision) and shorter time frames (a single sitting or a day or two) for a range of discipline-specific tasks, purposes, and audiences.

With planning, writing can become an authentic and integral part of every classroom. It's time to take some action . . .

Action Steps

1) At the beginning of the chapter, I describe a quick exercise I tried with my students to show how writing generates more writing. In the box below, at the top, write down your favorite food. Then, see what else comes to help you fill up that box:

2) Take a look at Table 6.1, a framework for writing across content areas.

   a. Which of these types of writing are you already using in your classroom? _____

   _____

   _____

   b. What type of writing is most prevalent in your classroom—daily, weekly, or unit/quarterly writing? Why do you think that is? _____

   _____

   _____

3) Which of the planning for instruction tenets—choice, audience, meaning, organization, and frequency—do you think you address well in your classroom? Why? Which do you think needs the most work? Why? _____

   _____

   _____

   _____

4) What formats and structures did I forget for your particular content area in Table 6.2?

   _____

   _____

   _____

Works Cited

Ausubel, D. P. (1969). *Educational psychology: A cognitive view*. New York, NY: Holt, Rinehart and Winston, Inc.

Bambrick-Santoyo, P., & Chiger, S. (2017). Until I write it down. *Educational Leadership, 74*, 46–50.

Education Trust. (2015,). *Checking in: Do classroom assignments reflect today's higher standards?* Retrieved from http://edtrust.org /wp-content/uploads/2014/09/CheckingIn_TheEducationTrust_Sept20152.pdf

Gallagher, K. (2017). The writing journey. *Educational Leadership, 74*, 24–29.

Fisher, D., Brozo, W., Frey, N., & Ivey, G. (2014). *50 instructional routines to develop content literacy* (3rd ed.). New York, NY: Pearson.

Langer, J., & Applebee, A. (1987). *How writing shapes thinking: A study of teaching of learning*. Urbana, IL: National Council of Teachers of English.

National Governors Association Center for Best Practices & Council of Chief State School Officers. (2010). *Common Core State Standards for English Language Arts*. Washington, DC: Authors.

National Writing Project & Nagin, C. (2006). *Because writing matters: Improving student writing in our schools*. New York, NY: Jossey-Bass.

Vacca, R., Vacca, J., & Mraz, M. (2013). *Content area reading: Literacy and learning across the curriculum* (11th ed.). New York, NY: Pearson.

Vermont Writing Collaborative (2016). A power tool: Writing based on knowledge and understanding. *American Educator, 40*, 33–38.

Chapter 7

Promote Daily Writing Strategies to Strengthen Thinking in the Discipline

Linda is a middle school science teacher who was bound and determined to make writing an integral part of her classroom. I walked into her room to find her at her desk, surrounded by stacks of paper. "This was not what I wanted!" she admonished me, gesturing at the piles of essays. "This is completely overwhelming!" I picked up a paper from the top of a stack. "What are these?" I asked, perusing a paper about the periodic table. "You said to write more, so I have been writing two- to five-page essays with my kids weekly. But I can't keep up with this." She looked at me over the papers with beseeching eyes: "Help!"

Why Is This Item on the List So Important?

I have found that when I mention the word "writing" to teachers outside of the English Language Arts, two words come to mind: report and essay. And that is exactly what Linda heard when she got word that I was offering a cross-curricular writing professional development session in her district. Before the professional development even happened, she began to assign weekly essays so that she could show me (and set an example for her colleagues) that writing can happen with ease in the science classroom. Instead, she was overwhelmed with grading, the writing process, grammar, and the sheer volume of papers that she found herself surrounded by on a weekly basis.

> *"Do this, not that" principle #6:* DO promote daily writing strategies to strengthen thinking in the discipline. DON'T write only "big" writing assignments once or twice a semester.

To Get Started

Why daily writing? I am afraid I have never been the type of person to jump into a body of water without testing the temperature first. I dip in my toes, I splash water on my legs—I need to get myself ready for full immersion! Daily writing is kind of like that—if we assign students major essays and reports without getting them "warmed up" to write, it is equivalent to pushing them off the high dive into a freezing, cold pool. Add to that the shock of writing in a class other than Language Arts—the horror! Having students regularly put pen/pencil to paper in all disciplines stops the shock-and-awe behavior.

Another reason to implement daily writing strategies is to lower the risk factor when writing. Big writing assignments are high risk—if done thoroughly, there is time and energy involved that requires an investment on the part of the student and the teacher. Daily writing strategies allow students to dabble in writing in the content (Wilfong, 2015). These lower-risk writing opportunities build the pathway for those later, higher-risk writing times.

Efferent versus aesthetic writing. In 1978, Louise Rosenblatt wrote about the transaction that happens between a reader and a text. Every time we read something, our reaction falls somewhere on a continuum between efferent (I learned something from this text!) to aesthetic (I love/hate this text!) (Rosenblatt, 1978). When students write, they often fall onto this same continuum—they are either writing to state facts (efferent) or to share an opinion (aesthetic). In content area writing, it is helpful to be very clear about what kind of writing we expect from our students—do we want them to write efferently and just show us what they learned? Or do we want them to write aesthetically and share their opinion? Or is it somewhere in the middle? To help combat this issue, I hang a continuum up in my room with a movable arrow on it. Any time we write in my classroom, I move the arrow to show students exactly what my expectation is for their writing—efferent, aesthetic, or somewhere in the middle. Figure 7.1 gives a sample writing continuum.

To help illustrate what I mean by this continuum, I often use a story about a car accident I was in: When the police officer put me in the back of the cruiser to tell my side of the accident, you better believe that I was as efferent as possible:

> "Officer, I was in the passing lane when the other driver side-swiped me."

Figure 7.1   Efferent/Aesthetic Writing Continuum

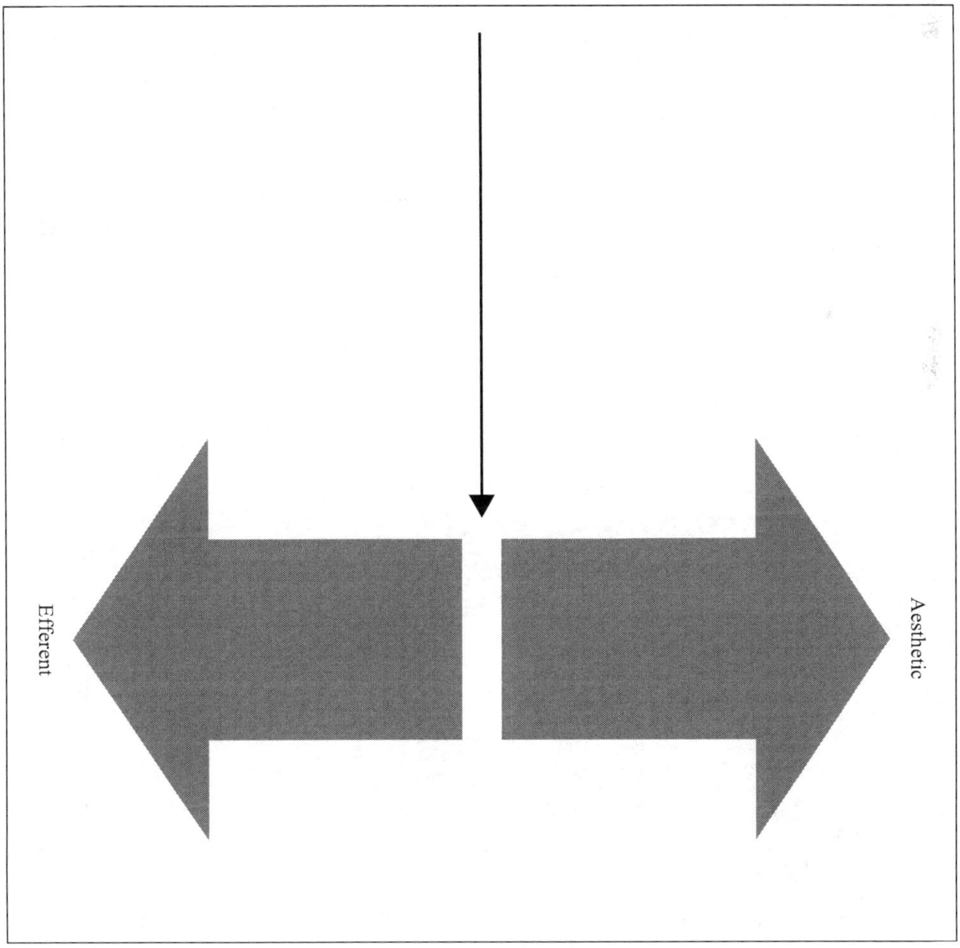

Table 7.1 Suggested Weekly Routine for Daily Writing

Day of the Week	Daily Writing Strategy
Monday	Quick write/journal prompt
Tuesday	Exit slip
Wednesday	Written conversations
Thursday	Entrance slip
Friday	Learning log

But, when I called my husband as I pulled away in my sad, scrapped-up car, I was pretty aesthetic: "Bob, you won't believe what happened! This terrible driver veered into my lane and totally messed my car."

After my example, I let students try it out. I lay out a scenario: A food fight in the lunch room. I divide students into three groups: Those that have to write out what happened for the principal (very efferent), those that have to call mom to tell what happened (efferent and aesthetic), and those who get to SnapChat, tweet, and text about what happened (very aesthetic—lots of hashtags!). This simple activity helps address audience, purpose, as well as teach about my expectations as a teacher of writers (and it is a ton of fun!).

The instructional updates presented in this chapter could easily become a routine that would allow a teacher to feel like they are supporting their students in everyday writing in all subjects. Table 7.1 presents a possible weekly calendar for daily writing.

Instructional Practices to Update

Updated Strategy #1: Using Entrance and Exit Slips to Get Students Thinking about Content through Written Expression

Entrance and exit slips were originally used as formative assessments; what did students learn from a previous class (entrance slips)? What did they learn at the end of a class (exit slips) (Furtak & Ruiz-Primo, 2008)? Yet both make excellent excuses for slipping some writing into the classroom that feels painless.

Traditional entrance and exit slips might ask students to sum up their learning in ten words or less (Wilfong, 2013), draw a picture to capture an important concept taught during a lesson, or even to tweet a summary of the class in 180 characters or less. But by taking this concept a step further,

Table 7.2   Possible Prompts for Entrance and Exit Slips

Entrance Slips	Exit Slips
◆ Name two things you already know about _____. ◆ What are two facts you remember from yesterday's class? ◆ Explain _____ to someone who has never heard of it before.	◆ Describe three things you took away from today's class. ◆ Write a three-sentence summary of the material presented in class today. ◆ Write a test question (multiple choice, short answer) over the material learned in class today

entrance and exit slips can be great practice for writing concisely and briefly about content-focused topics. Entrance slips get the juices flowing for learning that day, tapping into Goodman's theory of schema comprehension that brains must be "warmed up" for learning just like the body must be warmed up for exercise (Wilfong, 2013). Exit slips help the teacher and student see if learning took place. They alert an instructor to misconceptions—or even if that lesson was just "missed" by the student! Table 7.2 presents possible prompts for both entrance and exit slips.

A few ideas to keep in mind when presenting these entrance and exit slips to students:

- *Explicitly state that you expect complete sentences and proper sentence structure.* Students often feel that they are off the hook for clear communication in classes outside of Language Arts—let them know your expectations!

- *BUT, don't correct their mechanics, grammar, or sentence structure.* Your time is too valuable—use this to assess content, not writing ability. I do realize this contradicts the previous bullet point. But if the point of the exercise is low-risk writing and you return something as simple as an exit slip with corrections all over it, your students will be reluctant to take risks.

- *Make a clear grading system for yourself.* Too many entrance and exit slips can be overwhelming. I like to use a simple check plus, check, check minus so that I can grade these quickly.

In Chapter 5, I mentioned the use of the website Padlet to help students crowd-source vocabulary terms. Padlet is just as good for entrance and exit slips. At the beginning of class, a Padlet can be shared with a prompt that students can fill out via their "stickie." And at the end of class, a Padlet prompt can be used for students to type responses to an exit slip prompt. Figure 7.2 is

Figure 7.2 Snapshot of a Padlet Exit Slip

Lori Wilfong · + 15 · 2d

Writing group reflections

How did you feel about participating in a writing group today? Did you get usable feedback out of your participation?

Erica Roberts

I loved the writing groups we did today. Everyone's was personal in their own way and we were all to give great constructive criticism to help us make our papers the best they possibly could be. Reading our own stories aloud help ourselves find the little mistakes. I also felt that reading our own papers aloud let us put inflections where it was needed and that itself helped give the story its overall feel to really give it an impact.

Audrea Beamer

I enjoyed participating in the writing group today because I got feedback I wouldn't think of myself. Reading my story out loud also helped me to ckeck some mistakes in my writing.

Andrew Burwell

I enjoyed the writing group and being able to hear the stories of others. I received positive feedback which made the embarrassing story easier to review.

Amanda McCann

I really enjoyed doing the group reflection! I think it's best to hear yourself read your own writing to help find little mistakes. I also enjoyed my groups feedback!

Broc Siegenthaler

The writing group was a great experience for me because I got to read my story out loud to and get different feedback from everyone I'm my group. This helped me identify where I need to work on things that I didn't realize that I needed to work on.

Anna Lescallett

The writing group was very beneficial to me. It was interesting to see what stories everyone came up with. The feedback from peers is also helpful because they might have caught on to something that I did not notice before.

Brooke Jenkins

The writing group was beneficial to me because it made me feel more comfortable about the piece I chose to complete. Gaining feedback about both the story choice itself and things I need to add will hopefully make it turn out better than if I had not received any sort of critiquing. It was also fun to hear the pieces from others because they were full of homorous, and also chilling moments.

Cody Davis

I feel today's writing group experience was great. I got some good feedback on how to make my document more interesting and take it a little further. I believe it gave us a good base to reflect on eachothers work in a completely nonjudgmental way. I like the support I get from my peers and look forward to doing more activities like this in the future

Derek Mazak

I liked the writing group because got tons of feedback from multiple people. Also, I now feel like my writing is better than I originally thought.

Sophie Gough

I enjoyed participating in a writing group because I was able to see the reactions of my peers as I read my story aloud. I received reassurance that I was on the right track.

a snapshot of a Padlet that I did with a group of preservice teachers after they participated in their first writing group.

Updated Strategy #2: Implementing Prompts and Quick Writes to Draw Students into Writing about Content

Allowing students to write in response to prompts in the content area is a great way to promote reflection and prompt curiosity about upcoming topics (Fisher & Frey, 2008). But beyond basic engagement, it helps strengthen writing fluency in students, something some students struggle with beyond personal narrative writing (Fisher & Frey, 2013; Mason, Benedek-Wood, & Valasa, 2010). Think about it: When you ask a student to describe something that has happened to them personally, most can write and write. They are personally vested in the topic and they have much to say. But when you ask them to describe the different parts of a fraction, they struggle to make it sound like interesting prose.

Getting students used to writing on a variety of topics starts with the prompts that we give them. So many of the prompts we give to students are what I call finite—they are easily answered in one or two sentences and have a definite right or wrong answer (Wilfong, 2015). Finite prompts are great for entrance and exit slips. But infinite prompts, prompts that have more than one right answer and make it difficult to say "I'm done" at the end of a short writing time, promote fluent writing and student engagement (Wilfong, 2015).

To help teachers write better prompts, I like to use an old brainstorming strategy called RAFT. RAFT was traditionally used to help students think about who they were as the writer (Role), who they were writing for (Audience), what form the writing would take (Format), and what concept they were writing about (Topic) (Dean, 2006; Santa, Havens, & Valdes, 2004). However, when *teachers* use RAFT to draft their prompts for quick writes in their classroom, they are providing the tools students need to write successfully on nonfiction topics. Let's take a prompt commonly used in middle school social studies classrooms studying the American Revolution:

> *Name two reasons the colonists wanted to leave the rule of Great Britain.*

Can you guess how students responded to this very finite prompt? Most listed a reason or two (not in complete sentences, by the way) and then doodled until time was called. By using RAFT, we can turn this prompt into something a little more exciting:

Role	Audience	Format	Topic
Colonist	King of Great Britain	Letter	Reasons for establishing your own country

After using this graphic organizer, the teacher could post a prompt that reads like this: "You are a colonist who has decided to draft a letter to the King of Great Britain. In this letter, you will describe the many reasons why colonists wish to exit British rule and establish their own country." By using this graphic organizer, you are providing students with context, a place to hang their proverbial writing hats. So often, students stare blankly when given a writing prompt. But telling them who they are, who they are writing for, and what they are writing about, they are able to quickly get to work with a clear focus. A blank RAFT template is included at the end of this chapter to help you write better, more infinite prompts.

How long should students be given to respond to a prompt like this? My standard answer is seven minutes and forty-two seconds. Why? Five minutes is too short, ten minutes is too long, and seven minutes and forty-two seconds is too hard for students to figure out on the analog clock that is most likely hanging in your classroom (Wilfong, 2015).

These quickwrites can start discussion, lead into reading, or could be used to build a bigger essay at a later time.

Updated Strategy #3: Encouraging Students to Capture Learning through a Learning Log

A great end-of-the-week routine, learning logs help students reflect upon learning done over a longer period of time and capture it for future reflection (McDonald & Dominguez, 2009). Learning logs go beyond capturing data or recording facts for memorization (Klentschy, 2005); they ask students to dig deeply into their learning over the week, exercising their metacognitive muscles. A basic learning log might ask students to consider the following:

♦ What were three new concepts you learned this week?

♦ Find and describe one source that you might access to learn more about any of these topics (be specific!)

A more reflective learning log might ask students to respond to a few of the following prompts:

- What is something I discovered for the first time?
- What did I find that surprised me?
- What happened reminds me of . . .
- What am I wondering about now?

(McDonald & Dominguez, 2009)

These learning logs are great to use in those last frantic moments before the bell rings on a Friday. Put that youthful exuberance to good use by having them complete a weekly learning log, either in a notebook you can collect or through a Google Doc that can be added to week after week. Each week, you gather valuable data on your students' learning while providing low-risk ways for them to write in your content area. They get an actual record of their learning, valuable for them when answering the question, "What did you learn in school today?" I have even seen learning logs used to lead student-driven teacher—parent conferences!

Common Core Connection

The strategies presented in this chapter meet several of the writing standards presented in the Common Core State Standards for Literacy in History/ Social Studies, Science, & Technical Subjects.

Standards Addressed	Write routinely over extended time frames (time for reflection and revision) and shorter time frames (a single sitting or a day or two) for a range of discipline-specific tasks, purposes, and audiences.	Produce clear and coherent writing in which the development, organization, and style are appropriate to task, purpose, and audience.	Write informative/ explanatory texts, including the narration of historical events, scientific procedures/ experiments, or technical processes.	Introduce claim(s) about a topic or issue, acknowledge and distinguish the claim(s) from alternate or opposing claims, and organize the reasons and evidence logically.

Action Steps

Writing does not have to be major essays and reports that require tons of time assigning and grading! It is time to take some action . . .

1. Look at the content you have coming up in a few weeks. Draft the text for at least one entrance slip and one exit slip you could use with that content:

   Entrance slip: _____

   _____

   _____

   _____

   _____

   Exit slip: _____

   _____

   _____

   _____

   _____

2. Write two prompts that you could use during a specific part of an upcoming unit for quick writes (use the RAFT template at the end of the chapter to help you!):

   a. _____

   _____

   b. _____

   _____

Works Cited

Dean, D. (2006). *Strategic writing: The writing process and beyond in the secondary English classroom.* Urbana, IL: NCTE.

Fisher, D., & Frey, N. (2008). *Improving adolescent literacy: Content area strategies at work* (2nd ed.). Upper Saddle River, NJ: Pearson Prentice Hall.

Fisher, D., & Frey, N. (2013). A range of writing across the content areas. *The Reading Teacher, 67,* 96–101.

Furtak, E., & Ruiz-Primo, M. (2008). Making students' thinking explicit in writing and discussion: An analysis of formative assessment prompts. *Science Education, 92,* 792–824.

Klentschy, M. (2005). Science notebook essentials. *Science and Children, 43,* 24–27.

Mason, L., Benedek-Wood, E., & Valasa, L. (2010). Teaching low-achieving students to self-regulate persuasive quick write responses. *Journal of Adolescent and Adult Literacy, 53,* 303–312.

McDonald, J., & Dominguez, L. (2009). Reflective writing: Developing patterns for thinking about learning in science. *The Science Teacher, 76,* 46–49.

Rosenblatt, L. (1978). The transactional theory of reading and writing. In R. Ruddell & N. Unrau (Eds.), *Theoretical models and processes of reading* (5th ed., pp. 1363–1398). Newark, DE: International Reading Association.

Santa, C., Havens, L., & Valdes, B. (2004). *Project Criss: Creating independence through student-owned strategies.* Dubuque, IA: Kendall Hunt.

Wilfong, L. (2013). *Nonfiction strategies that work: Do this—not that!* New York, NY: Routledge.

Wilfong, L. (2015). *Writing strategies that work: Do this—not that!* New York: Routledge.

Role	Audience	Format	Topic

Complete prompt: _____

_____

_____

_____

♦ Possible formats: Wiki/Encyclopedia Entry, Interview, Summarize, Research Brief, Essay, Report, Speech, Letter, Brochure, News Article, Magazine Article, Picture Book, Autobiography, Biography, How-To Text, Pamphlet

Implement Slightly Larger Weekly Writing Strategies to Encourage Comprehension and Synthesis in the Discipline

The teacher held up a finger as I walked into the room. "Hold up," she said, typing away, "I want to capture what happened in my lesson today before I forget." I sat quietly while she typed furiously. "There!" she said triumphantly, closing her laptop. "I find it so important to summarize a lesson for myself before I move on." "That is awesome!" I responded eagerly. "Do you do that kind of thinking with the students?" She shook her head. "It's either essays or comprehension questions in here," she said shrugging her shoulders. "Is there anything in between?"

Why Is This Item on the List So Important?

Writing is like the reveal of a magician (Bambrick-Santoyo & Chiger, 2017). Through discussion, we get an idea of what some students think; through writing, thinking (or the lack thereof!) is immediately clear. What points do

I want to make? What ideas do I want to include—and leave out? These are questions every student asks themselves as they move towards writing that shows learning and logic.

To see if students "got" something, we do a number of things: ask questions to gauge comprehension (like in the scenario above), give a worksheet or graphic organizer for students to fill out, or require a visual to be created to show thinking. While these kinds of activities are okay, they don't build scholars of our content—they build students who memorize items for a test (or students who fake their way through *or* students who refuse to do inauthentic work). But the ultimate in sophistication in knowledge acquired is the ability to *write* and reflect about the topic (Bambrick-Santoyo & Chiger, 2017; Smith, Rook, & Smith, 2007). By allowing students to write a longer connected piece and reflect on their learning is the building of true independent thinkers (our ultimate goal as teachers!)

> *"Do this, not that" principle #8: DO implement slightly larger weekly writing strategies to encourage comprehension and synthesis in the discipline. DON'T write only "big" writing assignments once or twice a semester.*

To Get Started

Why Weekly Writing?

Somewhere between short, daily writing strategies and full-blown essays are weekly writings. I don't want to pigeon-hole these into saying they must follow a paragraph structure; I would rather state that these take longer than an everyday writing strategy (five minutes or less!) but nowhere near as long as a full essay.

The daily writing discussed in Chapter 7 allows students to flex their writing muscles in a way similar to the warm-ups an elite athlete might complete before a race. Fisher and Frey (2013) call these "power writings" and look on them as a way to build focus and fluency (Fisher & Frey, 2013). Continuing that analogy, weekly writing are the drills, scrimmages, and scenarios that same athlete might practice leading up to the game.

Weekly writing gives space for some of the repeated practice necessary for building up to more complex writing tasks (Lawrence, Galloway, Yim, & Lin, 2013). The analytic writing necessary for argumentative and informative genres needs to be broken down into smaller pieces to allow students time to refine and hone their craft. And like everyday writing, weekly writing gives a chance for every student to show their cards—what do they know about our content? Where are their misconceptions? By giving students time to write and reflect, they can't help but think more deeply about their learning (Gallagher, 2017; Smith et al., 2007).

Instructional Practices to Update

Updated Strategy #1: CREW-C Arguments

Structuring a good argument is hard for many students. While we can teach the Toulmin model and read and discuss editorials from a newspaper, so much of it comes back to the basic building blocks of argumentative writing.

Argument versus persuasive writing. When the Common Core Standards were first released, one of the biggest updates was the use of the word "argument" in place of "persuasion." To differentiate the two, I like to explain that argument is persuasion without the passion. In place of passion is evidence to support the claim.

A colleague, Andrew Pinney, and I first developed CREW as a reading tool (Wilfong, 2015). Students would read excellent arguments and then break them down into their building blocks: Claim, Reasons, Evidence, and Warrant. Table 8.1 gives a description of each part of the CREW acronym.

To update this strategy, especially for Grades 7 and above, we have added the counterclaim to the CREW (hence, the CREW-C). The counterclaim is a statement that refutes the original claim. In good argumentative writing, the author then tears down the counterclaim with evidence and/or reasons. Table 8.2 provides a sample CREW-C.

Students can write CREW-C about anything (snacks, sports, video games) but it can become a powerful, short writing strategy in content area

Table 8.1   CREW

CLAIM	A debatable and defensible statement.
REASON	A personal opinion or statement supporting the claim.
EVIDENCE	Credible fact, statistic, or idea (cited from a source) that supports the claim and reason.
WARRANT	The "why" statement, tying the whole argument together.

Table 8.2 CREW-C

CLAIM	Ohio is a great state.
REASON	One reason why it is a great state is because there is great beauty stemming from natural resources like Lake Erie.
EVIDENCE	According to www.daytrippers.com, Lake Erie offers a little something for everyone: roller coasters, islands, sandy and rocky beaches, and more!
WARRANT	If you are looking for a state with great natural resources, Ohio might be the state for you.
COUNTERCLAIM	There are others that might say that Indiana also offers great natural resources because it, too, borders a Great Lake. However, the shoreline of Indiana is much shorter in length than that of Lake Erie in Ohio. According to Ohio Sea Grant, Lake Erie has 262 miles of shoreline in Ohio, while Lake Michigan only has 42 miles of shoreline in Indiana.

classrooms. Using the CREW-C template (included at the end of the chapter), students can structure a supported argument in any discipline, perfect for Socratic Seminar, debates, or Bracket Battles, described below.

Updated Strategy #2: Bracket Battles

Nikki was so excited it was like she was bursting! "You know that Bracket Battle activity you did with us?" she asked, referring to a strategy I introduced to a group of teachers at a National Writing Project professional development session. I nodded and she continued: "That strategy is the reason why my students did so well on the state test," she said. "My co-teacher said it really taught students to argue and back themselves up with evidence."

I first wrote about Bracket Battles in 2015 and love them with a passion. Game-ifying anything is such a fun way to draw students into reading and writing.

In a Bracket Battle, students are seeded on a March Madness-like bracket. There is an umbrella topic for the debate (like important inventors, figures of the 20th century, or best book read), under which students choose or are assigned a specific topic. Figure 8.1 shows a sample Bracket Battle around iconic scientists.

Students are given a short amount of time to research and prepare an argument about their topic. Structure for their argument comes in the form of the CREW-C, described above. Decisions have to be made—what evidence should be used in the first round? If a student throws down their best

Figure 8.1   Iconic Scientist Bracket Battle

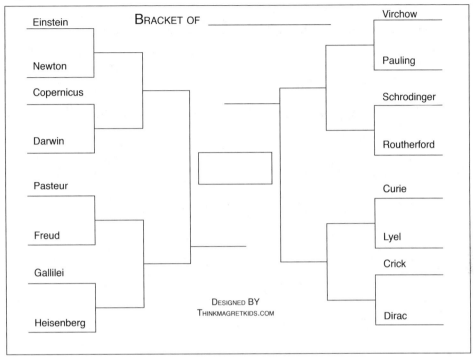

evidence in the opening round, they are left with weak evidence for later rounds, great practice for writing longer argumentative essays.

When the Bracket Battle begins, arguments are presented and then the rest of the class votes about who moves on to the next round. But don't worry! If Newton beats Einstein (as seeded in Figure 8.1), the student who battled for Einstein doesn't sit idly by and watch the rest of the battle. When Newton gears up to write their next CREW-C for the Elite 8, Einstein joins his or her team and helps them formulate their next argument. This keeps happening until the final round when the whole half of the bracket (or class) is battling the other half.

To update this strategy, my colleague Andrew Pinney once again thought of a way to bring more accountability to the voting during the Bracket Battle. Too often, students would vote for their friend or for the best delivery and not on who had the best evidence or counterclaim. To that end, he developed a rubric for students to use to take notes on the CREW-C that each student presented. The rubric included a points value that made it clear, when tallied, which individual or team deserved the vote to move on in the Bracket Battle. Figure 8.2 presents the Bracket Battle rubric (a full template of both the Bracket Battle template and the rubric are included at the end of the chapter).

The use of the rubric helps students pay attention to the nuances of argument. The repetition of writing and delivering the arguments help

Figure 8.2 Bracket Battle Rubric

Bracket Battle Rubric – Team #1 _____

		3	2	1
Claim/ Argument				Introduces a claim about the topic
Reason #1 (with evidence)	Reasons:	Reason AND evidence clearly supports the claim	Reason OR evidence supports the claim	Reason/evidence is not provided or does not support the claim
Reason #2 (with evidence)	Reasons:	Reason AND evidence clearly supports the claim	Reason OR evidence supports the claim	Reason/evidence is not provided or does not support the claim
Reason #3 (with evidence)	Reasons	Reason AND evidence clearly supports the claim	Reason OR evidence supports the claim	Reason/evidence is not provided or does not support the claim

Argument #1 Against opponent	Reasons:	Reasons AND evidence negate the opponents claim	Reasons OR evidence negate the opponent's claim	Reasons/ evidence is not given nor negates the opponent's claim
Argument #2 Against opponent	Reasons:	Reasons AND evidence negate the opponent's claim	Reasons OR evidence negate the opponent's claim	Reasons/ evidence is not given nor negates the opponent's claim
Total Score				_____/16

students refine their argumentative craft. And on top of it all, this strategy is simply a blast.

A word to the wise—everyone loves this strategy. If you present this to a group of a teachers on your team, they will all want to try it. Chemistry teachers will battle which element on the periodic table is superior, American History teachers will battle for the president with the most lasting legacy—the battles can go on forever. Space battles out over the calendar year. As with any good strategy, students will tire of it eventually!

Updated Strategy #3: Found Poetry

Summary writing is a legitimate weekly writing and a skill that many students need help refining. Two summary strategies, The Most Important Thing and Somebody Wanted But So Then, are included back in Chapter 2. This strategy, Found Poetry, is an "outside-the-box" summary strategy that really shows what a student knows about content in a creative way.

Both a comprehension strategy and a writing strategy, Found Poetry empowers students to "find" poetry in prose. Ask a student to write a poem over a textbook chapter or informational article—the groans will be heard across the school! But show a student how they can boil down prose to its essence to create a poem using the author's words, and you have created poets! Here are the steps to use Found Poetry:

1. After reading a text (a chapter or an article work best), students select a connected, 100-word passage from the text that contains the central idea or most important point by the author.

2. The 100-word passage is copied either onto a piece of a paper or typed into a document on the computer (hint: the computer makes this strategy go much faster!).

3. Begin to extract all but the most important words. Articles like "the," conjunctions like "and" are out of here. Each sentence is scrutinized for all but the most pressing words.

4. To keep students on their toes, I will often tell them that they have $1.00 to spend and every word kept is a nickel. The dismissal of unimportant words becomes easier when money is involved (even pretend money)!

5. Once the purge has happened, students rearrange the words into poetic form. This is where the magic happens—what was once a piece of prose suddenly becomes a poem.

(adapted from Dunning & Stafford, 1992)

Figure 8.3 presents the process of Found Poetry, from the original, 100-word passage identified as central to a nonfiction text, followed by the

Figure 8.3 Found Poetry Example

Extra ducks in the canoe? A preseason deer hanging behind the shed? Si will find it, helping
Fairbanks enforce the state's conservation laws. "I take him in the boat or canoe, out in the four-
wheeler, wherever I go," Fairbanks said. "He's not aggressive at all with other dogs."

But Si is also trained to protect his handler, and he was pre-selected for police work even as a
puppy to be an eager and aggressive dog.

"They are very high energy. They really don't make great house pets," Fairbanks said. "They're
great with my kids … they can pull on his ears and pull his tail and stick their hands into his
mouth and he doesn't care a bit. But you can't leave him at home alone or he'd tear the house up.
He needs to burn that energy off every day."

(Excerpted from Myers, 2018)

Extra ducks ~~in the canoe?~~ ~~A~~ preseason deer ~~hanging behind the shed?~~ Si will find it, ~~helping~~
~~Fairbanks enforce the state's conservation laws.~~ ~~"I take him in the~~ boat or canoe, ~~out in the~~ four-
wheeler, ~~wherever I go," Fairbanks said. "He's~~ not aggressive ~~at all with other dogs."~~

~~But~~ Si ~~is also~~ trained to protect ~~his handler, and he was~~ pre-selected for police work ~~even as a~~
~~puppy to be an eager and aggressive dog.~~

~~"They are very~~ high energy. ~~They really don't make great house pets,"~~ ~~Fairbanks said. "They're~~
great with ~~my~~ kids ~~… they can~~ pull on his ears ~~and~~ pull his tail ~~and~~ stick ~~their~~ hands into his
mouth ~~and~~ he doesn't care ~~a bit. But you~~ can't leave him ~~at home~~ alone ~~or he'd~~ tear the house up.
~~He~~ needs to burn ~~that~~ energy off ~~every day."~~

Extra ducks?
Preseason deer?
Si will find it
Boat, canoe, four-wheeler
Not aggressive
Si trained to protect
Pre-selected for police work
High energy
Great with kids
Pull on his ears
Pull his tail
Stick hands into his mouth
He doesn't care
Can't leave him alone
Tear the house up
Needs to burn energy off

process of discarding unimportant/irrelevant words, to the resulting piece of found poetry.

Found Poetry takes modeling, time, and practice but eventually, it becomes many students' favorite way of identifying the main idea, summarizing, and writing poetry about (sometimes dry) topics. A few favorite ways that I have seen this strategy in action is to jigsaw different sections of a text (students write and share Found Poetry with each other), to summarize a textbook or novel chapter—even to boil down court cases to their essence in an American government class!

Common Core Connection

The strategies presented in this chapter meet several of the writing standards and one of the reading standards presented in the Common Core State Standards for Literacy in History/Social Studies, Science, & Technical Subjects.

Writing Standards (History/Social Studies/Science/Other Technical Subjects)

6–8	9–10	11–12

6–8.1 Write arguments focused on *discipline-specific content*.
  6–8.1a Introduce claim(s) about a topic or issue, acknowledge and distinguish the claim(s) from alternate or opposing claims, and organize the reasons and evidence logically.
  6–8.1b Support claim(s) with logical reasoning and relevant, accurate
	9–10.1 Write arguments focused on *discipline-specific content*.
	  9–10.1a Introduce precise claim(s), distinguish the claim(s) from alternate or opposing claims, and create an organization that establishes clear relationships among the claim(s), counterclaims, reasons, and evidence.
		11–12.1 Write arguments focused on *discipline-specific content*.
		  11–12.1a Introduce precise, knowledgeable claim(s), establish the significance of the claim(s), distinguish the claim(s) from alternate or opposing claims, and create an organization that logically sequences the claim(s), counterclaims, reasons, and evidence.

(Continued)

(Continued)

6–8	9–10	11–12
data and evidence that demonstrate an understanding of the topic or text, using credible sources. 6–8.1c Use words, phrases, and clauses to create cohesion and clarify the relationships among claim(s), counterclaims, reasons, and evidence. 6–8.1d Establish and maintain a formal style. 6–8.1e Provide a concluding statement or section that follows from and supports the argument presented. 6–8.2 Write informative/explanatory texts, including the narration of historical events, scientific procedures/ experiments, or technical processes. 6–8.2a Introduce a topic clearly, previewing what is to follow; organize ideas, concepts, and information into broader categories as appropriate to achieving purpose; include formatting (e.g., headings), graphics (e.g., charts, tables), and multimedia when useful to aiding comprehension.	9–10.1b Develop claim(s) and counterclaims fairly, supplying data and evidence for each while pointing out the strengths and limitations of both claim(s) and counterclaims in a discipline-appropriate form and in a manner that anticipates the audience's knowledge level and concerns. 9–10.1c Use words, phrases, and clauses to link the major sections of the text, create cohesion, and clarify the relationships between claim(s) and reasons, between reasons and evidence, and between claim(s) and counterclaims. 9–10.1d Establish and maintain a formal style and objective tone while attending to the norms and conventions of the discipline in which they are writing. 9–10.1e Provide a concluding statement or section that follows from or supports the argument presented. 9–10.2 Write informative/ explanatory texts, including the narration	11–12.1b Develop claim(s) and counterclaims fairly and thoroughly, supplying the most relevant data and evidence for each while pointing out the strengths and limitations of both claim(s) and counterclaims in a discipline-appropriate form that anticipates the audience's knowledge level, concerns, values, and possible biases. 11–12.1c Use words, phrases, and clauses as well as varied syntax to link the major sections of the text, create cohesion, and clarify the relationships between claim(s) and reasons, between reasons and evidence, and between claim(s) and counterclaims. 11–12.1d Establish and maintain a formal style and objective tone while attending to the norms and conventions of the discipline in which they are writing. 11–12.1e Provide a concluding statement or section that follows from or supports the argument presented.

6–8	9–10	11–12
6–8.2b Develop the topic with relevant, well-chosen facts, definitions, concrete details, quotations, or other information and examples. 6–8.2c Use appropriate and varied transitions to create cohesion and clarify the relationships among ideas and concepts. 6–8.2d Use precise language and domain-specific vocabulary to inform about or explain the topic. 6–8.2e Establish and maintain a formal style and objective tone. 6–8.2f Provide a concluding statement or section that follows from and supports the information or explanation presented. 6–8.4 Produce clear and coherent writing in which the development, organization, and style are appropriate to task, purpose, and audience. 6–8.5 With some guidance and support from peers and adults, develop and strengthen writing as needed by planning, revising, editing, rewriting, or trying a new approach,	of historical events, scientific procedures/experiments, or technical processes. 9–10.2a Introduce a topic and organize ideas, concepts, and information to make important connections and distinctions; include formatting (e.g., headings), graphics (e.g., figures, tables), and multimedia when useful to aiding comprehension. 9–10.2b Develop the topic with well-chosen, relevant, and sufficient facts, extended definitions, concrete details, quotations, or other information and examples appropriate to the audience's knowledge of the topic. 9–10.2c Use varied transitions and sentence structures to link the major sections of the text, create cohesion, and clarify the relationships among ideas and concepts. 9–10.2d Use precise language and domain-specific vocabulary to manage the complexity of the topic and convey a style appropriate to the discipline and	11–12.2 Write informative/explanatory texts, including the narration of historical events, scientific procedures/experiments, or technical processes. 11–12.2a Introduce a topic and organize complex ideas, concepts, and information so that each new element builds on that which precedes it to create a unified whole; include formatting (e.g., headings), graphics (e.g., figures, tables), and multimedia when useful to aiding comprehension. 11–12.2b Develop the topic thoroughly by selecting the most significant and relevant facts, extended definitions, concrete details, quotations, or other information and examples appropriate to the audience's knowledge of the topic. 11–12.2c Use varied transitions and sentence structures to link the major sections of the text, create cohesion, and clarify the relationships among complex ideas and concepts.

(*Continued*)

(Continued)

6–8	9–10	11–12
focusing on how well purpose and audience have been addressed. 6–8.6 Use technology, including the Internet, to produce and publish writing and present the relationships between information and ideas clearly and efficiently. 6–8.7 Conduct short research projects to answer a question (including a self-generated question), drawing on several sources and generating additional related, focused questions that allow for multiple avenues of exploration. 6–8.8 Gather relevant information from multiple print and digital sources, using search terms effectively; assess the credibility and accuracy of each source; and quote or paraphrase the data and conclusions of others while avoiding plagiarism and following a standard format for citations. 6–8.9 Draw evidence from informational texts to support analysis, reflection, and research. 6–8.10 Write routinely over extended time frames (time for	context as well as to the expertise of likely readers. 9–10.2e Establish and maintain a formal style and objective tone while attending to the norms and conventions of the discipline in which they are writing. 9–10.2f Provide a concluding statement or section that follows from and supports the information or explanation presented (e.g., articulating implications or the significance of the topic). 9–10.4 Produce clear and coherent writing in which the development, organization, and style are appropriate to task, purpose, and audience. 9–10.5 Develop and strengthen writing as needed by planning, revising, editing, rewriting, or trying a new approach, focusing on addressing what is most significant for a specific purpose and audience. 9–10.6 Use technology, including the Internet, to produce, publish, and update individual or shared	11–12.2d Use precise language, domain-specific vocabulary and techniques such as metaphor, simile, and analogy to manage the complexity of the topic; convey a knowledgeable stance in a style that responds to the discipline and context as well as to the expertise of likely readers. 11–12.2e Provide a concluding statement or section that follows from and supports the information or explanation provided (e.g., articulating implications or the significance of the topic). 11–12.4 Produce clear and coherent writing in which the development, organization, and style are appropriate to task, purpose, and audience. 11–12.5 Develop and strengthen writing as needed by planning, revising, editing, rewriting, or trying a new approach, focusing on addressing what is most significant for a specific purpose and audience.

6–8	9–10	11–12
reflection and revision) and shorter time frames (a single sitting or a day or two) for a range of discipline-specific tasks, purposes, and audiences.	writing products, taking advantage of technology's capacity to link to other information and to display information flexibly and dynamically. 9–10.7 Conduct short as well as more sustained research projects to answer a question (including a self-generated question) or solve a problem; narrow or broaden the inquiry when appropriate; synthesize multiple sources on the subject, demonstrating understanding of the subject under investigation. 9–10.8 Gather relevant information from multiple authoritative print and digital sources, using advanced searches effectively; assess the usefulness of each source in answering the research question; integrate information into the text selectively to maintain the flow of ideas, avoiding plagiarism and following a standard format for citation.	11–12.6 Use technology, including the Internet, to produce, publish, and update individual or shared writing products in response to ongoing feedback, including new arguments or information. 11–12.7 Conduct short as well as more sustained research projects to answer a question (including a self-generated question) or solve a problem; narrow or broaden the inquiry when appropriate; synthesize multiple sources on the subject, demonstrating understanding of the subject under investigation. 11–12.8 Gather relevant information from multiple authoritative print and digital sources, using advanced searches effectively; assess the strengths and limitations of each source in terms of the specific task, purpose, and audience; integrate information into the text selectively to maintain the flow

(Continued)

6–8	9–10	11–12
	9–10.9 Draw evidence from informational texts to support analysis, reflection, and research. 9–10.10 Write routinely over extended time frames (time for reflection and revision) and shorter time frames (a single sitting or a day or two) for a range of discipline-specific tasks, purposes, and audiences.	of ideas, avoiding plagiarism and overreliance on any one source and following a standard format for citation. 11–12.9 Draw evidence from informational texts to support analysis, reflection, and research. 11–12.10 Write routinely over extended time frames (time for reflection and revision) and shorter time frames (a single sitting or a day or two) for a range of discipline-specific tasks, purposes, and audiences.
RST.6–8.2 Analyze content-area-specific text development. Determine the central ideas or conclusions of a text. Provide an accurate and objective summary that includes the central ideas or conclusions of the text.	RST.9–10.2 Analyze content-area-specific text development. a. Determine the central ideas or conclusions of a text. b. Provide an accurate and objective summary of the central ideas of the text that traces the text's explanation or depiction of a complex process, phenomenon, or concept.	RST.11–12.2 Analyze content-area-specific text development. a. Determine the central ideas or conclusions of a text. b. Provide an objective summary of the central ideas of a text, paraphrasing complex concepts, processes, or information by presenting them in simpler but still accurate terms.

Action Steps

Weekly writing strategies like these can become an integral part of every classroom! It's time to take some action . . .

1) Take a look at the strategies from Chapter 7 along with the strategies presented here in Chapter 8. Make a plan for implementing daily and weekly writing across a week you have coming up in your school year.

Day of the Week	Writing Strategy
Monday	
Tuesday	
Wednesday	
Thursday	
Friday	

2) Write a CREW-C for your content area:

CLAIM	
REASON	
EVIDENCE	
WARRANT	
COUNTERCLAIM	

3) Think of an umbrella topic for a Bracket Battle in your classroom. Then, brainstorm 16 different topics to prepare for a battle!

Umbrella topic: _____

Topic #1:	Topic #2:
Topic #3:	Topic #4:
Topic #5:	Topic #6:
Topic #7:	Topic #8:
Topic #9:	Topic #10:
Topic #11:	Topic #12:
Topic #13:	Topic #14:
Topic #15:	Topic #16:

4) Bonus! Try a piece of Found Poetry with a text you plan to read with your students. What did you think of the strategy? Could you see yourself trying it with your students in the future?

_____

_____

_____

_____

Works Cited

Bambrick-Santoyo, P., & Chiger, S. (2017). Until I write it down. *Educational Leadership, 74,* 46–50.

Dunning, S., & Stafford, W. (1992). *Getting the knack: 20 poetry writing exercises.* Urbana, IL: National Council of Teachers of English.

Fisher, D., & Frey, N. (2013). A range of writing across the content areas. *The Reading Teacher, 67,* 96–101.

Gallagher, K. (2017). The writing journey. *Educational Leadership, 74,* 24–29.

Lawrence, J., Galloway, E., Yim, S., & Lin, A. (2013). Learning to write in middle school? Insights into adolescent writers' instructional experiences across content areas. *Journal of Adolescent and Adult Literacy, 57,* 151–161.

Myers, J. (2018, September 26). Newsela | From missing kids to extra fish, Minnesota K-9 team is on the job. Retrieved September 26, 2018, from https://newsela.com/read/elem-conservation-k-9-team-minnesota/id/45901/

Smith, K., Rook, J., & Smith, T. (2007). Increasing student engagement: Effective metacognitive writing strategies in content areas. *Preventing School Failure, 51,* 43–48.

Wilfong, L. (2015). *Writing strategies that work: Do this—not that!* New York, NY: Routledge.

CREW-C Template

CLAIM	
REASON	
EVIDENCE	
WARRANT	
COUNTERCLAIM	

Bracket Battle Template

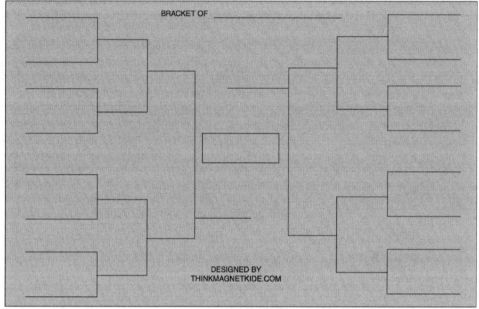

BRACKET OF _____

DESIGNED BY
THINKMAGNETKIDE.COM

Bracket Battle Rubric – Team #1 _____

		3	2	1
Claim/ Argument				Introduces a claim about the topic
Reason #1 (with evidence)	Reasons:	Reason AND evidence clearly supports the claim	Reason OR evidence supports the claim	Reason/evidence is not provided or does not support the claim
Reason #2 (with evidence)	Reasons:	Reason AND evidence clearly supports the claim	Reason OR evidence supports the claim	Reason/evidence is not provided or does not support the claim
Reason #3 (with evidence)	Reasons	Reason AND evidence clearly supports the claim	Reason OR evidence supports the claim	Reason/evidence is not provided or does not support the claim

Argument #1 Against opponent	Reasons:	Reasons AND evidence negate the opponents claim	Reasons OR evidence negate the opponent's claim	Reasons/ evidence is not given nor negates the opponent's claim
Argument #2 Against opponent	Reasons:	Reasons AND evidence negate the opponent's claim	Reasons OR evidence negate the opponent's claim	Reasons/ evidence is not given nor negates the opponent's claim
Total Score				_____/16

Chapter 9

Plan and Teach One "Big" Informational Piece Per Semester

"Let me ask you a question", Ms. G. said to me during a team meeting. "I do lab reports; are lab reports informational writing?" I considered her question but before I could speak, Mr. O'Connor, next to me, piped up: "Yes, but also, no." We all looked at him. "Well, for sure students are writing up what happened during a lab in an informational way, but don't you use kind of a question–response format?" Ms. G. nodded her head. "So, it isn't connected text," Mr. O'Connor went on. "It's basically like comprehension questions. For a real piece of informational writing, it needs to be like an essay, right?" They all looked at me for confirmation. "Well, yes, but also no," was my unhelpful response. "I think we want to help students work beyond a basic lab report to something a little meatier, maybe once a semester."

Why Is This Item on the List So Important?

Informational writing gets a bad rap. If I say "informational writing" aloud to teachers, most conjure up visions of research reports, term papers, and five-paragraph essays—and groan. While perhaps not as alluring as its opinion/argument writing counterpart, informational writing can help students adopt the scholarly stance that proves that they are experts of a topic or content area.

Most little kids we know become experts of something—dinosaurs, planets, ocean life. And they can't wait to spew that information all over someone (anyone!) who is willing to listen about the plates that covered the stegosaurus. Informational writing can recapture that enthusiasm that children have, allowing students to share a topic that they are passionate about through writing.

> "Do this, not that" principle #9: DO plan and teach one "big" informational piece per semester. DON'T assign a vague informational research report.

To Get Started

Before we dive into strategies and formats to breathe life into informational writing, we have to pull back a bit and talk about some basics. At the heart of writing is the writing process. It applies to all writing, but especially becomes of emphasis when we talk about longer pieces, like those described here in Chapter 9 and later in Chapter 10. The section that follows on the writing process applies to all genres: narrative, informative, and argumentative/opinion writing.

The writing process. The writing process is composed of five distinct processes. They are presented in Figure 9.1.

Figure 9.1   The Writing Process

Brainstorming At the beginning of the writing process is brainstorming. Putting pencil to paper, cursor to screen, this allows students to plan what they are going to write. This could be a bulleted list, outline, t-chart—really anything that helps a student think about the content and organization of their soon-to-be-constructed paper. Two words to the wise when it comes to brainstorming:

- Not everything that is brainstormed needs to be turned into a paper and taken through the rest of the writing process (Gallagher & Kittle, 2018). Having a place to dabble in the various genres taught in class and to generate a ton of ideas allows students to get into a writerly stance without risk—a journal or notebook, or special GoogleDoc page can all give students space to brainstorm.

- Brainstorms shouldn't be graded. Seriously, how can you grade someone's ideas in the infancy stage? Give credit for participation, if needed, but refrain from assigning points to something that is being developed.

Drafting. At some point, a student chooses something from their brainstorming and develops it into a full paper. It is tempting to take these drafts home, edit, and assign some sort of a grade, but don't! A draft is a jumping-off point for students to start think seriously about their content—if you take the paper and slash your red pen through it at this point, you are not teaching the student anything about writing (but getting plenty of writing practice, yourself). Instead, give points for a completed draft and move onto revision.

When you assign a completed draft to students, they are probably going to ask how long that draft should be (that sentence sounded an awful lot like *If You Give a Mouse a Cookie*). Rather than give a sentence, paragraph, or page minimum, give students a rubric or checklist before they begin drafting. Anytime you give a minimum, the majority of students will only write to that minimum. By refraining from giving any kind of length requirements, you are priming students to decide for themselves when something is done (or not).

Revising. Revision is focused on content. As a content area teacher, you are now thinking about what is required for the finished piece to sound like it belongs to the discipline—what are the pieces and parts of a lab report that is written up as a research brief? When analyzing a primary source, what vocabulary needs to be included? How is a paper in your content area organized? *These* are the kind of lessons you need to show your students. Choose a handful of these ideas and show students how to incorporate these into their own work.

Table 9.1 Basic Conventions Rubric

2	1	0
Over the course of the paper, only minor errors exist in spelling, capitalization, punctuation, and grammar.	Over the course of the paper, some errors exist in spelling, capitalization, punctuation, and grammar but do not majorly impede the message.	Over the course of the paper, major errors exist in spelling, capitalization, punctuation, and grammar that majorly impede the message.

Editing. Editing focuses on the conventions and mechanics of correctly written English. It is usually this part of the writing process that throws non-English/Language Arts teachers; I'm not an English teacher—how can I be expected to teach grammar, punctuation, and spelling? The answer? *You're not.* Revision is at the heart of the writing process (Calkins, 1986). The focus of the content area teacher needs to be on what content should be included in a paper related to your discipline and in what format it should be presented. The only requirement in this part of the writing process for content area teachers is that you do ask students to communicate clearly, which includes conventional spelling, capitalization, spelling, and grammar. Rather than spend time correcting these issues, a simple rubric can be used to assess this aspect of their work, presented in Table 9.1.

Publishing. At the end of the writing process is publication. Submitting and celebrating the end of a piece cements the use of such an assignment in your classroom!

Instructional Practices to Update

Updated Strategy #1: Applying Authentic Reasons and Formats for Informational Writing

As stated in the anecdote at the beginning of the chapter, a laboratory report is an authentic reason for informational writing in science. But, as also pointed out in that anecdote, watering down a lab report to filling out a worksheet takes away some of the authenticity. Table 9.2 presents the reasons for informational writing across disciplines.

Table 9.2 Reasons for Informational Writing across Disciplines

Content Area	Reasons for Informational Writing
Social Studies	*Corroborating*—Comparing and contrasting points of view *Contextualizing*—Placing a document or idea into historical context (date, place, events) *Tracing*—Describing events across a time period *Problem-solving*—Laying out a historical problem and offering solutions *The Ripple Effect*—Examining the effect of decisions on historical/political/geographical contexts *Biography*—Describing impactful individuals
Science	*Corroborating*—Comparing and contrasting points of view *Contextualizing*—Placing a scientific idea into a historical context (date, place, events) *Tracing*—Describing the evolution of a scientific idea or invention across a time period OR describing the testing of a hypothesis in a laboratory format *Problem-solving*—Laying out a scientific problem and offering solutions *Explore*—How the world works and connects, physically and biologically *The Ripple Effect*—Examining the effect of scientific decisions on humans and/or the environment *Biography*—Describing impactful individuals
Math	*Corroborating*—Comparing and contrasting points of view *Contextualizing*—Placing a mathematical idea into historical context (date, place, events) *Tracing*—Describing the evolution of a mathematical idea across a time period *Problem-solving*—Laying out a mathematical problem and offering solutions *Biography*—Describing impactful individuals
Art/Music	*Corroborating*—Comparing and contrasting points of view *Contextualizing*—Placing an artistic or musical idea into historical context (date, place, events) *Tracing*—Describing the evolution of an artistic or music movement *Biography*—Describing impactful individuals *Connect*—Draw connections between pieces among artists or musicians
Language Arts	*All of the above can be completed in an ELA classroom!*

Figure 9.2 Possible Formats for Informational Writing

Document-based questions   Speech   Social Media Post   Newspaper Article   Research brief   Infographic   Pamphlet   Brochure   Text Conversation   Play/Readers' Theatre

Once an authentic reason for writing is established, students can choose or be assigned a format. Think outside the five-paragraph box here! Figure 9.2 has a list of possible formats for informational writing that can cross disciplines.

With any format a student chooses or is assigned to use, examples must be given. Called a mentor text, these models allow students to see how a historian, scientist, or mathematician applies this format (Culham, 2014; Pytash & Morgan, 2014).

Updated Strategy #2: Placing Meaningful Opportunities for Informational Writing in Your Curriculum

The biggest frustration that I have encountered with content area teachers when it comes to infusing more writing into the curriculum is the time factor—there is never enough! To make writing meaningful in your content area, you have to choose the right topic. What is a unit in your curriculum where further exploration is warranted? What is a topic in your curriculum where a bigger idea is explored (like The Revolutionary War) and what are several sub-topics that could be researched by students (like the African American experience, the women's role, etc.)?

To combat the time factor, I have developed a writing unit template specifically for content area teachers, based my previous work on writing units for English teachers (Wilfong, 2015). Figure 9.3 presents a blank template for this writing unit (a complete template is included at the end of the chapter). This template can be used for any genre of writing but works especially well for the two that are designated for content area teachers: informative and argumentative writing.

Remember the quick write strategy from Chapter 7 where you had your students write for seven minutes and forty-two seconds? Those become more purposeful within the structure of this writing unit. Rather

Figure 9.3 Blank Writing Unit Template

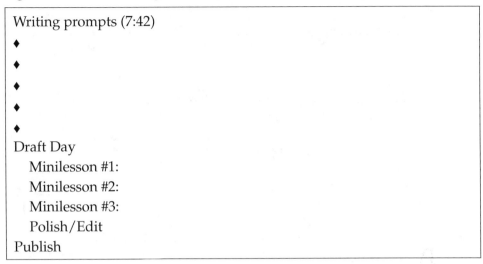

Writing prompts (7:42)

◆

◆

◆

◆

◆

Draft Day

   Minilesson #1:

   Minilesson #2:

   Minilesson #3:

   Polish/Edit

Publish

than assigning random prompts, the prompts become focused on the topic and the informational writing genre. The template above has space for five prompts—as many as are warranted can be given. One prompt is given each day, every other day, once a week—whatever works for you! These can be sprinkled throughout your instruction and hands-on time within your classroom as you see fit. Once at least five of these prompts have been given (my rule of thumb for finding a piece that actually merits finishing), students go back through their beginnings and select one to take to a completed draft, in a format that is assigned by the teacher or chosen by the student. I call this process "Draft Day" because it has two meanings—they are "drafting" which piece they want to finish and then they are actually finishing a rough draft.

Once that draft is complete, revision begins. As a content area teacher, you get to decide what students need to know to be excellent writers of your discipline. Called minilessons, you select a small number of strategies to show students how to make their paper better. These minilessons do not come out of thin air—they come from the standards! Table 9.3 presents the informational writing standards by grade band.

To identify minilessons, I take a hard look at the standards for my grade band and highlight the individual minilessons I see embedded in the

Table 9.3 Informational Writing Standards by Grade Band

6–8	9–10	11–12
6–8.2 Write informative/ explanatory texts, including the narration of historical events, scientific procedures/ experiments, or technical processes. 　6–8.2a Introduce a topic clearly, previewing what is to follow; organize ideas, concepts, and information into broader categories as appropriate to achieving purpose; include formatting (e.g., headings), graphics (e.g., charts, tables), and multimedia when useful to aiding comprehension. 　6–8.2b Develop the topic with relevant, well-chosen facts, definitions, concrete details, quotations, or other information and examples. 　6–8.2c Use appropriate and varied transitions to create cohesion and 　clarify the relationships among ideas and concepts. 　6–8.2d Use precise language and domain-specific vocabulary	9–10.2 Write informative/ explanatory texts, including the narration of historical events, scientific procedures/ experiments, or technical processes. 　9–10.2a Introduce a topic and organize ideas, concepts, and information to make important connections and distinctions; include formatting (e.g., headings), graphics (e.g., figures, tables), and multimedia when useful to aiding comprehension. 　9–10.2b Develop the topic with well-chosen, relevant, and sufficient facts, extended definitions, concrete details, quotations, or other information and examples appropriate to the audience's knowledge of the topic. 　9–10.2c Use varied transitions and sentence structures to link the major sections of the text, create cohesion, and clarify the relationships among ideas and concepts.	11–12.2 Write informative/ explanatory texts, including the narration of historical events, scientific procedures/ experiments, or technical processes. 　11–12.2a Introduce a topic and organize complex ideas, concepts, and information so that each new element builds on that which precedes it to create a unified whole; include formatting (e.g., headings), graphics (e.g., figures, tables), and multimedia when useful to aiding comprehension. 　11–12.2b Develop the topic thoroughly by selecting the most significant and relevant facts, extended definitions, concrete details, quotations, or other information and examples appropriate to the audience's knowledge of the topic. 　11–12.2c Use varied transitions and sentence structures to link the major sections of the text, create cohesion, and clarify the relationships

6–8	9–10	11–12
to inform about or explain the topic.6–8.2e Establish and maintain a formal style and objective tone. 6–8.2f Provide a concluding statement or section that follows from and supports the information or explanation presented.	9–10.2d Use precise language and domain-specific vocabulary to manage the complexity of the topic and convey a style appropriate to the discipline and context as well as to the expertise of likely readers. 9–10.2e Establish and maintain a formal style and objective tone while attending to the norms and conventions of the discipline in which they are writing. 9–10.2f Provide a concluding statement or section that follows from and supports the information or explanation presented (e.g., articulating implications or the significance of the topic).	among complex ideas and concepts. 11–12.2d Use precise language, domain-specific vocabulary and techniques such as metaphor, simile, and analogy to manage the complexity of the topic; convey a knowledgeable stance in a style that responds to the discipline and context as well as to the expertise of likely readers. 11–12.2e Provide a concluding statement or section that follows from and supports the information or explanation provided (e.g., articulating implications or the significance of the topic).

standards. Figure 9.4 presents the six to eight Informational Writing standards, with individual minilessons bulleted.

Using Figure 9.4, I can identify 12 minilessons that I could teach students about how to become great informational writers—yikes! Because of the time factor, I ask content area teachers to select *three* that they feel are most important to their discipline. Does your discipline introduce the topic in a very specific way? Select that to show students. Is precise language important to conveying information about the topic? Select that to show students. The point is that you do not have to try to go through every minilesson identified by the standards with writing in your content area—be selective! By

Figure 9.4   Grades 6–8 Informational Writing Standards with Minilessons

6-8.2 Write informative/explanatory texts, including the narration of historical events, scientific procedures/ experiments, or technical processes.

6-8.2a
- Introduce a topic clearly, previewing what is to follow.
- Organize ideas, concepts, and information into broader categories as appropriate to achieving purpose.
- Include formatting (e.g., headings), graphics (e.g., charts, tables), and multimedia when useful to aiding comprehension.

6-8.2b
- Develop the topic with relevant, well-chosen facts,
- definitions,
- concrete details,
- quotations,
- or other information and examples.

6-8.2c
- Use appropriate and varied transitions to create cohesion and clarify the relationships among ideas and concepts.

6-8.2d
- Use precise language and domain-specific vocabulary to inform about or explain the topic.

6-8.2e
- Establish and maintain a formal style and objective tone.

6-8.2f
- Provide a concluding statement or section that follows from and supports the information or explanation presented.

narrowing down your focus to a few key points, you have also narrowed down the grading of this piece. If you teach a minilesson on a topic (say, formal style) then you will read the paper for formal style in your discipline and grade it accordingly.

I keep throwing out that word—minilesson. Chapter 10 will include a thorough description of what a minilesson is and a sample minilesson.

Once you have taught your minilessons, I like to give a day for students to polish up their drafts. Publication happens when these are submitted. Celebrate! You have made your students true scholars of your discipline!

Updated Strategy #3: Fusing Narrative into Nonfiction

As you look through these last two chapters, you will realize that narrative is not mentioned. When the Common Core Standards were published, narrative was not one of the genres designated for content area teachers to use in their classrooms; the focus was solely on informational and opinion (K-5)/argumentative (6–12) writing. Yet, several teachers have described to me engaging projects that they have used in their classrooms to bring narrative elements to informational writing in the content area classrooms. I describe two of them here:

♦ In a chemistry class, one teacher wanted to bring a little pizazz to the study of the periodic table. "I've had them write descriptions and analysis of how the elements of the periodic table interact," she told me, "but I knew there had to be something better out there." Building on the idea that elements are classified into families and that when elements bond they share electrons, she decided to have students create comic or picture books about these relationships: "It always made sense in my head that these relationships were almost like dating or siblings! So writing stories about them was a logical next step." Students developed their plot lines and then infused facts about each of the elements to show their knowledge. Deep descriptions of covalent bonds were included, per the rubric. On submission day, the teacher was not sure what she would get. She had modeled the process by writing her own picture book and gave time in class, and was delighted to see how engaged the students were in the writing. She was overwhelmed by the result: "The books turned out so well. The biggest hurdle was not the infusion of the facts; they were awesome at that! They were more worried about their drawing skills and used different computer applications for their illustrations." Her favorite part of the project? "The day after the books were due, we took a quick test over covalent bonds and the periodic table. Kids *aced* it. This is a project that I will do year after year."

♦ To bring Westward Expansion to life, a history teacher wanted to go beyond a chronological description. "Part of our nation's history are the stories people tell about settling the west. I wanted to capture students' imaginations." To that end, he had students research the identity of a teenager that made the journey with their family. As a class, they studied the hardships these settlers faced as they made their way across America and settled into frontier towns. "From there, I had students write diary entries, using the identity of the person they had researched." Like the chemistry teacher above, this teacher had students infuse facts from their whole class research into their diary entries. "I just expected kids to write or type these on regular paper. One student got the idea to make it into a real diary, with handwriting, and dirty pages and everything and before you knew it, everyone was outside, stomping on paper in the dirt." He, too, was thrilled with the end result: "The students really got Westward Expansion. In my end-of-the-year surveys, more than 80% of my students wrote about this project." To update the project for the upcoming year, this teacher is using 7:42s to help the students begin to craft their diary entries over the course of the Westward Expansion unit.

Common Core Connection

The strategies presented in this chapter target the informational writing standards presented in the Common Core State Standards for Literacy in History/Social Studies, Science, & Technical Subjects.

Writing Standards (History/Social Studies/Science/Other Technical Subjects)

6–8	9–10	11–12
6–8.2 Write informative/ explanatory texts, including the narration of historical events, scientific procedures/ experiments, or technical processes.	9–10.2 Write informative/ explanatory texts, including the narration of historical events, scientific procedures/ experiments, or technical processes.	11–12.2 Write informative/ explanatory texts, including the narration of historical events, scientific procedures/ experiments, or technical processes.
6–8.2a Introduce a topic clearly, previewing what is to follow; organize ideas, concepts, and information into	9–10.2a Introduce a topic and organize ideas, concepts, and information to make important connections and distinctions;	11–12.2a Introduce a topic and organize complex ideas, concepts, and information so that each new element

6-8	9-10	11-12
broader categories as appropriate to achieving purpose; include formatting (e.g., headings), graphics (e.g., charts, tables), and multimedia when useful to aiding comprehension. 6–8.2b Develop the topic with relevant, well-chosen facts, definitions, concrete details, quotations, or other information and examples. 6–8.2c Use appropriate and varied transitions to create cohesion and clarify the relationships among ideas and concepts. 6–8.2d Use precise language and domain-specific vocabulary to inform about or explain the topic. 6–8.2e Establish and maintain a formal style and objective tone. 6–8.2f Provide a concluding statement or section that follows from and supports the information or explanation presented. 6–8.4 Produce clear and coherent writing in which the development, organization, and style are appropriate to task, purpose, and audience.	include formatting (e.g., headings), graphics (e.g., figures, tables), and multimedia when useful to aiding comprehension. 9–10.2b Develop the topic with well-chosen, relevant, and sufficient facts, extended definitions, concrete details, quotations, or other information and examples appropriate to the audience's knowledge of the topic. 9–10.2c Use varied transitions and sentence structures to link the major sections of the text, create cohesion, and clarify the relationships among ideas and concepts. 9–10.2d Use precise language and domain-specific vocabulary to manage the complexity of the topic and convey a style appropriate to the discipline and context as well as to the expertise of likely readers. 9–10.2e Establish and maintain a formal style and objective tone while attending to the norms and conventions of the discipline in which they are writing.	builds on that which precedes it to create a unified whole; include formatting (e.g., headings), graphics (e.g., figures, tables), and multimedia when useful to aiding comprehension. 11–12.2b Develop the topic thoroughly by selecting the most significant and relevant facts, extended definitions, concrete details, quotations, or other information and examples appropriate to the audience's knowledge of the topic. 11–12.2c Use varied transitions and sentence structures to link the major sections of the text, create cohesion, and clarify the relationships among complex ideas and concepts. 11–12.2d Use precise language, domain-specific vocabulary and techniques such as metaphor, simile, and analogy to manage the complexity of the topic; convey a knowledgeable stance in a style that responds to the discipline and context as well as to the expertise of likely readers.

(Continued)

(Continued)

6–8	9–10	11–12
6–8.5 With some guidance and support from peers and adults, develop and strengthen writing as needed by planning, revising, editing, rewriting, or trying a new approach, focusing on how well purpose and audience have been addressed. 6–8.6 Use technology, including the Internet, to produce and publish writing and present the relationships between information and ideas clearly and efficiently. 6–8.7 Conduct short research projects to answer a question (including a self-generated question), drawing on several sources and generating additional related, focused questions that allow for multiple avenues of exploration. 6–8.8 Gather relevant information from multiple print and digital sources, using search terms effectively; assess the credibility and accuracy of each source; and quote or paraphrase the data and conclusions	9–10.2f Provide a concluding statement or section that follows from and supports the information or explanation presented (e.g., articulating implications or the significance of the topic). 9–10.4 Produce clear and coherent writing in which the development, organization, and style are appropriate to task, purpose, and audience. 9–10.5 Develop and strengthen writing as needed by planning, revising, editing, rewriting, or trying a new approach, focusing on addressing what is most significant for a specific purpose and audience. 9–10.6 Use technology, including the Internet, to produce, publish, and update individual or shared writing products, taking advantage of technology's capacity to link to other information and to display information flexibly and dynamically. 9–10.7 Conduct short as well as more sustained research projects to answer	11–12.2e Provide a concluding statement or section that follows from and supports the information or explanation provided (e.g., articulating implications or the significance of the topic). 11–12.4 Produce clear and coherent writing in which the development, organization, and style are appropriate to task, purpose, and audience. 11–12.5 Develop and strengthen writing as needed by planning, revising, editing, rewriting, or trying a new approach, focusing on addressing what is most significant for a specific purpose and audience. 11–12.6 Use technology, including the Internet, to produce, publish, and update individual or shared writing products in response to ongoing feedback, including new arguments or information. 11–12.7 Conduct short as well as more sustained research projects to answer a question (including a self-generated

6–8	9–10	11–12
of others while avoiding plagiarism and following a standard format for citations.

6–8.9 Draw evidence from informational texts to support analysis, reflection, and research.

6–8.10 Write routinely over extended time frames (time for reflection and revision) and shorter time frames (a single sitting or a day or two) for a range of discipline-specific tasks, purposes, and audiences. | a question (including a self-generated question) or solve a problem; narrow or broaden the inquiry when appropriate; synthesize multiple sources on the subject, demonstrating understanding of the subject under investigation.

9–10.8 Gather relevant information from multiple authoritative print and digital sources, using advanced searches effectively; assess the usefulness of each source in answering the research question; integrate information into the text selectively to maintain the flow of ideas, avoiding plagiarism and following a standard format for citation.

9–10.9 Draw evidence from informational texts to support analysis, reflection, and research.

9–10.10 Write routinely over extended time frames (time for reflection and revision) and shorter time frames (a single sitting or a day or two) for a range of discipline-specific tasks, purposes, and audiences. | question) or solve a problem; narrow or broaden the inquiry when appropriate; synthesize multiple sources on the subject, demonstrating understanding of the subject under investigation.

11–12.8 Gather relevant information from multiple authoritative print and digital sources, using advanced searches effectively; assess the strengths and limitations of each source in terms of the specific task, purpose, and audience; integrate information into the text selectively to maintain the flow of ideas, avoiding plagiarism and overreliance on any one source and following a standard format for citation.

11–12.9 Draw evidence from informational texts to support analysis, reflection, and research.

11–12.10 Write routinely over extended time frames (time for reflection and revision) and shorter time frames (a single sitting or a day or two) for a range of discipline-specific tasks, purposes, and audiences. |

Action Steps

Informational writing can become every student's favorite project in your class! It's time to take some action . . .

1) As a writer yourself, what part of the writing process is most challenging for you? Why do you think that is? _____

_____

_____

_____

2) Examine the tables that give purposes and formats for informational writing in the content area. Which do you think match best with the curriculum you teach? Why? _____

_____

_____

_____

3) Meaningful information writing requires a great umbrella topic with smaller issues or topics underneath it that students can explore. What is an umbrella topic in your curriculum that lends itself well to informational writing? _____

4) What are five writing prompts (7m:42s) that you could use to help students write about the above topic (or subtopics)?

   ♦ _____

   _____

   ♦ _____

   _____

   ♦ _____

   _____

   ♦ _____

   _____

   ♦ _____

   _____

Works Cited

Calkins, L. (1986). *The art of teaching writing*. Portsmouth, NH: Heinemann.

Culham, L. (2014). *The writing thief*. Portsmouth, NH: Stenhouse.

Gallagher, K., & Kittle, P. (2018). *180 Days:Two teachers and the quest to engage and empower adolescents*. Portsmouth, NH:Heinemann.

Pytash, K., & Morgan, D. (2014). Using mentor texts to teach writing in science and social studies. *The Reading Teacher*, *68*, 93–102.

Wilfong, L. (2015). *Writing strategies that work: Do this—not that!* New York, NY: Routledge.

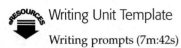 Writing Unit Template

Writing prompts (7m:42s)

♦

♦

♦

♦

♦

Draft Day

Minilesson #1:

Minilesson #2:

Minilesson #3:

Polish/Edit

Publish

Chapter 10

Plan and Teach One "Big" Argumentative Piece Per Semester

"Now you want us to do arguments?" a teacher asked me during a professional development session. "I feel like we've got informational writing down; this is overkill." As a social studies teacher, with a state end-of-course exam, she was feeling frustrated. "I need a real reason to have students argue about something in my class." Her neighbor elbowed her: "Social studies is all argument. Everything we teach could be positioned as an argument." She sat straight up. "I guess I never thought of it like that."

Why Is This Item on the List So Important?

The ability to argue effectively is so important that claims were made when the Common Core Standards came out that this, along with the ability to support that claim with evidence, are the two most important standards.

Our students are opinionated. They share these opinions widely on social media—everything from their favorite musicians, sport stars, and fashion are argued on Twitter, Instagram, and Snapchat. Finding ways to harness their predilection for argument into coherent papers shouldn't be difficult—but it is! Part of this goes back to the idea of authenticity—arguing about something that you do not care about is hard. When you really care about something, you will work to prove you are right. One of my undergraduate students proved this to me last year—she was great at narrative writing but arguing was just not a natural part of her sweet demeanor. However, when I told her that new rap wasn't my thing, she saw red! "Dr. Wilfong," she huffed, "Drake is amazing! I'm going to prove it to you!" For her argumentative paper, she laid out and supported a passionate claim supporting Drake over my personal favorite, Dr. Dre. While I didn't cede the point (90s West Coast rap rules!), I had to give her credit—I definitely gave Drake a serious listen because of her.

In my mind, argumentative writing goes hand and hand with discussion. Arguments are meant to be had out loud! As you plan argumentative writing in your classroom, think about how you can either start or end with your writing discussion and debate—Socratic Seminars and Bracket Battles lend themselves well to making argumentative writing come alive!

> "Do this, not that" principle #9: DO plan and teach one "big" argumentative piece per semester. DON'T assign a vague argumentative paper.

To Get Started

Lauren was trying to convince me that Drake bested Dr. Dre because she was passionate about his music. While I explained earlier that argumentative writing is persuasion without the passion, it was the passion that drove Lauren to write that paper! To create great argumentative writers, we need to tap into the foundation of analysis:

1. Passion: When a student cares, it shows. Getting investment into a topic is key to hooking argumentative writers.
2. Ideas: Honing in on what really matters is tough. Yes, Lauren liked Drake because she thought he was cute, but when it came down to it, his music spoke to her life. His lyrics mattered to her. Her argument was that much more solid because she focused in on an idea that she could truly write a claim about, give good reasons, and offer credible evidence.

3. Structure: Our passion and ideas are nothing without a structure to help us organize our thoughts. Just like with informational writing, we need formats (beyond the five-paragraph essay!) that help us express our arguments ably.

4. Authority: No one can argue well without building expertise on their topic. Students need time to read deeply on their topic to have the facts and evidence necessary to support their claim.

(Marchetti & O'Dell, 2018)

Instructional Practices to Update

Updated Strategy #1: Finding Authentic Reasons for Argumentative Writing

As mentioned above, authenticity is key to getting students to want to engage in argumentative writing and speaking. There are issues in our disciplines that are not up for debate—the Holocaust is not up for debate in social studies nor is climate change challenged in scientific communities (Ehrenworth, 2017). I was recently in a classroom that debated whether igneous rock was superior to metamorphic. The arguments were lackluster because at the heart of it, the argument lacked controversy.

Where does controversy live in your discipline? Table 10.1 presents a sampling of controversial topics ripe for argumentative writing across the content areas.

Like informational writing, a good argument doesn't always lend itself to a simple five-paragraph essay. Figure 10.1 presents possible formats for argumentative writing.

Updated Strategy #2: Creating Minilessons to Assist Students in Revision

Once students have a draft (ungraded, except for completion), it is time to show them how to make their papers better. As mentioned in Chapter 9, minilessons are standards-based lessons that help students improve the content of their papers. The key part of the word "minilesson" is the "mini"—these lessons are designed to last 10–12 minutes to allow students ample time to

Table 10.1 Controversial Topics for Argumentative Writing Across Content Areas

Content Area	Controversial Topics
Social Studies	Was [westward expansion/exploration/ World War I], overall, a force for good?
	Athens versus Sparta: Which is a better model for today's youth?
	Columbus/Julius Caesar: hero or villain?
	Under what conditions should child soldiers receive amnesty?
	Was the American Revolution "radical"—did it change conditions overall for many people?
	Was the U.S. Civil War won more through strategy, supplies, or ideas?
Science	Which NASA proposal should be funded: space stations, asteroid mining, or terraforming?
	Bottled water versus clean tap water: Which should the United Nations fund abroad?
	Bio-engineered food sources: Encourage and fund them or ban them?
	Renewable energy: Which should we invest in: wind, solar, or hydro?
	What is the best way to limit climate change: control carbon emissions, limit greenhouse gases, or . . .?
	Epidemiology: Which virus is most likely the cause of ___?
	Should we protect wolves [or bears] in state parks?
Art/ Music	What artistic movement had the biggest impact on art/music in this country?
	In _____ symphony, which instrument provides the pivotal sound?
	What artist can be pointed to as a major modern influence?
Language Arts	*Language Arts: Literature*
	Is [a fictional character] weak or strong?
	Is this story more about ___ or ___?
	Does the author develop the mood more through ___ or through ___?
	Which character has the greater impact on events: ___ or ___?
	In this story, does the setting shape the character more, or the character shape the setting?

Content Area	Controversial Topics
	Language Arts: Nonfiction Are zoos good or bad for endangered animals? Should we have animals in classrooms? Are rats friend or foe to humans? Are competitive sports a force for good in schools? Should kids be allowed to play violent role-playing games?

(Adapted from Ehrenworth, 2017)

Figure 10.1 Possible Formats for Argumentative Writing

Document-Based Questions   Speech   Social Media Post   Newspaper Article
Infographic   Pamphlet   Brochure   Text Conversation
Play/Readers' Theatre   Editorial   Rant   Blog post

apply the instructional concept to their own paper (Calkins, 1986). Minilessons are the difference between assigning writing and actually teaching writing. Here are the steps to writing your own minilessons:

1. *Focus on one small part of a standard.* As illustrated in Chapter 9, there are a lot of minilessons embedded in the standards. Choose one small topic (not a whole standard!) for instructional focus.

2. *Quickly define/describe the focus for students.* Simply naming and defining the focus can help clarify for both you and the students exactly what change you are hoping them to make in their papers.

3. *Model the change in a piece of writing.* I am going to ask something big of you here: You need to have something written to use as part of the minilesson. In order for students to see what kind of change you want them to make in their own writing, you need to show them *how* to do this. Take writing a claim, for instance. You can tell a student how to write a claim until you are blue in the face. But until you stand in front of them and show them a claim you have written, in your content area, and then show them how to make it better, it is just talk.

4. *Guide practice.* In small groups, allow students to practice the minilesson on a sample piece of writing.

5. *Independent practice.* Students can now try their own hand at applying the minilesson to their paper.

Figure 10.2 presents a blank minilesson template (a full template is included at the end of the chapter). Figure 10.3 presents a completed minilesson that

Figure 10.2 Blank Minilesson Template

Genre:
Complete standard:
Portion of standard for focus:
Define/Describe:
Modeling:
Guided Practice:
Independent Practice:

Figure 10.3 Completed Minilesson

Genre: Argumentative **Complete Standard:** 6-8.1a Introduce claim(s) about a topic or issue, acknowledge and distinguish the claim(s) from alternate or opposing claims, and organize the reasons and evidence logically.
Portion of Standard for Focus: Introduce claim(s) about a topic or issue
Define/Describe: "Students, as we learned during our Bracket Battle, a claim needs to be debatable and defensible to be worthy of arguing. Today we are going to focus in on the claim of your papers. There are three major types of claims: Fact, Value, and Policy. (A handout for the three major types of claims is included at the end of the chapter).
Modeling: Present an introductory paragraph to students from a paper you have written. Be sure that it isn't perfect – we want to make it better! "Students, here is a claim for a paper I am writing about _____." I need to check it for a few things: Is my stance clear – do you know what side I am on? Do I give away all of my evidence in my claim? And, have I used terms like 'I think' or 'I feel?'" After a little discussion, model adjusting your claim based on one of these three attributes.
Guided Practice: In small groups, present some basic claims to students on unrelated topics. Have them evaluate the claims based on those three attributes: ♦ Is the writer's stance clear? ♦ Are terms like "I think" or "I feel" used? ♦ Is all evidence given away in the claim? Students can adjust the claim based on those criteria while you circulate to check for understanding.
Independent Practice: Have students evaluate their own claims using the criteria presented during modeling and guided practice. Circulate to talk to students about their adjustments as needed.

could be used in your own classroom in conjunction with argumentative writing!

Minilessons are hard to make "mini" at first. As you become more adept at modeling, and guided practice, you will notice that your minutes spent teaching start to shrink—that's exactly what you want! I always tell teachers at the beginning of the writing process to remember this: The most important thing in writing with students is that you teach them something and then they have time to apply that to their writing. Without that time to apply the minilesson to their own writing, it is just direct instruction.

Updated Strategy #3: Flash Debates and Bracket Battles to Spur Argumentative Writing

As I mentioned at the beginning of the chapter, I believe that argumentative writing is uniquely suited to discussion. It makes sense—a debate is not something that is supposed to be one-sided! Bringing speaking and listening into the fold either before or after writing will help to strengthen your students' arguments.

We learned about Bracket Battles in Chapter 8. Teachers report having students write bigger papers on both sides of the Bracket Battle. A Bracket Battle can be used before writing the bigger paper to excite students to engage in argumentative writing (there is nothing more motivating than losing—I have watched students lose the initial Bracket Battle and then go research their topic to the bone to write a thorough argument to prove their point). Using the Bracket Battle as weekly writing before writing the bigger paper also allows students to build on their shorter arguments.

After writing a paper, a Bracket Battle allows students to show off their research and writing skills because they are so prepared for the oral arguments. Time between rounds is shortened because students have all of their evidence right in front of them.

Ehrenworth (2017) likes the use of a Flash Debate prior to engaging in argumentative writing. By allowing students to test the waters of logic and reasoning, we are preparing them for the bigger task of organizing a longer paper (Kuhn, Hemberger, & Khait, 2016). Unlike a Bracket Battle, a Flash Debate is only done in partners (not in front of the whole class). One question is posed to students. Each student takes a side and then debates each other based on previous study of the topic and background knowledge. The teacher circulates to check on argumentative style—are they using a claim? Reasons? Evidence (Ehrenworth, 2017)?

When I tried this out with a group of sixth graders recently, I learned that I had to time the Flash Debates. Students quickly ran through their ideas and no real "debate" happened; it was more of a Think—Pair—Share than a debate. I began setting a timer for one minute and told the partners to designate one student as the first to speak. When the timer began, the first partner had to speak for the full minute, referring to notes and ideas to sustain talk. When the timer went off they would wipe their brows before the other partner began talking. Once both had presented their sides, I set the timer for 30 seconds to allow the first speaker to counter their partner. We switched sides and did it again. Success!

You can see a logical progression that might develop here—start with CREW-C. Move into Flash Debates. Write argumentative papers stemming from the Flash Debates. Finish with a Bracket Battle!

Common Core Connection

The strategies presented in this chapter target the argumentative writing standards presented in the Common Core State Standards for Literacy in History/Social Studies, Science, & Technical Subjects.

Writing Standards (History/Social Studies/Science/Other Technical Subjects)

6–8	9–10	11–12

6–8.1 Write arguments focused on *discipline-specific content*.
  6–8.1a Introduce claim(s) about a topic or issue, acknowledge and distinguish the claim(s) from alternate or opposing claims, and organize the reasons and evidence logically.
  6–8.1b Support claim(s) with logical reasoning and relevant, accurate data and evidence that demonstrate an understanding of the topic or text, using credible sources.
	9–10.1 Write arguments focused on *discipline-specific content*.
	  9–10.1a Introduce precise claim(s), distinguish the claim(s) from alternate or opposing claims, and create an organization that establishes clear relationships among the claim(s), counterclaims, reasons, and evidence.
	  9–10.1b Develop claim(s) and counterclaims fairly, supplying data and evidence for
		11–12.1 Write arguments focused on *discipline-specific content*.
		  11–12.1a Introduce precise, knowledgeable claim(s), establish the significance of the claim(s), distinguish the claim(s) from alternate or opposing claims, and create an organization that logically sequences the claim(s), counterclaims, reasons, and evidence.
		  11–12.1b Develop claim(s) and counterclaims fairly and thoroughly,

6–8	9–10	11–12
6–8.1c Use words, phrases, and clauses to create cohesion and clarify the relationships among claim(s), counterclaims, reasons, and evidence. 6–8.1d Establish and maintain a formal style. 6–8.1e Provide a concluding statement or section that follows from and supports the argument presented. 6–8.4 Produce clear and coherent writing in which the development, organization, and style are appropriate to task, purpose, and audience. 6–8.5 With some guidance and support from peers and adults, develop and strengthen writing as needed by planning, revising, editing, rewriting, or trying a new approach, focusing on how well purpose and audience have been addressed. 6–8.6 Use technology, including the Internet, to produce and publish writing and present the relationships between information and ideas clearly and efficiently. 6–8.7 Conduct short research projects to	each while pointing out the strengths and limitations of both claim(s) and counterclaims in a discipline-appropriate form and in a manner that anticipates the audience's knowledge level and concerns. 9–10.1c Use words, phrases, and clauses to link the major sections of the text, create cohesion, and clarify the relationships between claim(s) and reasons, between reasons and evidence, and between claim(s) and counterclaims. 9–10.1d Establish and maintain a formal style and objective tone while attending to the norms and conventions of the discipline in which they are writing. 9–10.1e Provide a concluding statement or section that follows from or supports the argument presented. 9–10.4 Produce clear and coherent writing in which the development, organization, and style are appropriate to task, purpose, and audience.	supplying the most relevant data and evidence for each while pointing out the strengths and limitations of both claim(s) and counterclaims in a discipline-appropriate form that anticipates the audience's knowledge level, concerns, values, and possible biases. 11–12.1c Use words, phrases, and clauses as well as varied syntax to link the major sections of the text, create cohesion, and clarify the relationships between claim(s) and reasons, between reasons and evidence, and between claim(s) and counterclaims. 11–12.1d Establish and maintain a formal style and objective tone while attending to the norms and conventions of the discipline in which they are writing. 11–12.1e Provide a concluding statement or section that follows from or supports the argument presented. 11–12.4 Produce clear and coherent writing in which the

(Continued)

6–8	9–10	11–12
answer a question (including a self-generated question), drawing on several sources and generating additional related, focused questions that allow for multiple avenues of exploration. 6–8.8 Gather relevant information from multiple print and digital sources, using search terms effectively; assess the credibility and accuracy of each source; and quote or paraphrase the data and conclusions of others while avoiding plagiarism and following a standard format for citations. 6–8.9 Draw evidence from informational texts to support analysis, reflection, and research. 6–8.10 Write routinely over extended time frames (time for reflection and revision) and shorter time frames (a single sitting or a day or two) for a range of discipline-specific tasks, purposes, and audiences.	9–10.5 Develop and strengthen writing as needed by planning, revising, editing, rewriting, or trying a new approach, focusing on addressing what is most significant for a specific purpose and audience. 9–10.6 Use technology, including the Internet, to produce, publish, and update individual or shared writing products, taking advantage of technology's capacity to link to other information and to display information flexibly and dynamically. 9–10.7 Conduct short as well as more sustained research projects to answer a question (including a self-generated question) or solve a problem; narrow or broaden the inquiry when appropriate; synthesize multiple sources on the subject, demonstrating understanding of the subject under investigation.	development, organization, and style are appropriate to task, purpose, and audience. 11–12.5 Develop and strengthen writing as needed by planning, revising, editing, rewriting, or trying a new approach, focusing on addressing what is most significant for a specific purpose and audience. 11–12.6 Use technology, including the Internet, to produce, publish, and update individual or shared writing products in response to ongoing feedback, including new arguments or information. 11–12.7 Conduct short as well as more sustained research projects to answer a question (including a self-generated question) or solve a problem; narrow or broaden the inquiry when appropriate; synthesize multiple sources on the subject, demonstrating understanding of the subject under investigation.

6–8	9–10	11–12
	9–10.8 Gather relevant information from multiple authoritative print and digital sources, using advanced searches effectively; assess the usefulness of each source in answering the research question; integrate information into the text selectively to maintain the flow of ideas, avoiding plagiarism and following a standard format for citation. 9–10.9 Draw evidence from informational texts to support analysis, reflection, and research. 9–10.10 Write routinely over extended time frames (time for reflection and revision) and shorter time frames (a single sitting or a day or two) for a range of discipline-specific tasks, purposes, and audiences.	11–12.8 Gather relevant information from multiple authoritative print and digital sources, using advanced searches effectively; assess the strengths and limitations of each source in terms of the specific task, purpose, and audience; integrate information into the text selectively to maintain the flow of ideas, avoiding plagiarism and overreliance on any one source and following a standard format for citation. 11–12.9 Draw evidence from informational texts to support analysis, reflection, and research. 11–12.10 Write routinely over extended time frames (time for reflection and revision) and shorter time frames (a single sitting or a day or two) for a range of discipline-specific tasks, purposes, and audiences.

Action Steps

Let's tap into students' natural ability to argue! It's time to take some action . . .

1) Add to Table 10.1—What are some other controversial topics that you can think of that can help students authentically argue in your content area?

_____

_____

_____

_____

2) What do you find most intimidating about the minilesson process? Why?

_____

_____

_____

3) Would Flash Debates work to help spur your students toward argumentative writing? Why or why not? _____

_____

_____

_____

Works Cited

Calkins, L. (1986) *The art of teaching writing*. Portsmouth, NH: Heinemann.

Ehrenworth, M. (2017). Why argue? Language arts, science, social studies, mathematics—the craft of argumentation belongs in every discipline. *Educational Leadership, 74*, 35–40.

Kentucky Writing Project (2018). Take a stand. Retrieved from www.kentuckywritingproject.com/claims.html.

Kuhn, D., Hemberger, L., & Khait, V. (2016). *Argue with me: Argument as a path to developing students' thinking and writing* (2nd ed.). New York, NY: Routledge.

Marchetti, A., & O'Dell, R. (2018). *Beyond literary analysis: Teaching students to write with passion and authority about any texts*. Portsmouth, NH: Heinemann.

Wilfong, L. (2015). *Writing strategies that work: Do this—not that!* New York: Routledge.

Minilesson Template

Genre:
Complete Standard:
Portion of Standard for Focus:
Define/Describe:
Modeling:
Guided Practice:
Independent Practice:

FACT (writer is trying to prove something is true)	**IS or IS NOT** **ARE or ARE NOT**	**Fast food is unhealthy.**
VALUE **(requires writer to share or establish criteria)**	BETTER/BEST, MORE/ LESS, WORSE/WORST —IER or—IEST words	Tacos are a healthier choice than hamburgers.
POLICY (writer is trying to change the way things are)	SHOULD/SHOULD NOT	Schools should serve healthier foods.

(Adapted from the Kentucky Writing Project, 2018)